The Top
Ninja
Air Fryer

UK Cookbook

365 Days Delicious and Crispy Air Fryer Recipes with Easy to Follow Instructions for Beginners

Kenneth B. Delorme

Table of Contents

Chapter 5 Poultry 24

Chapter 6 Fish and Seafood 30

Chapter 7 Beef, Pork, and Lamb 35

Chapter 8 Pizzas, Wraps, and Sandwiches

Chapter 9 Vegetables and Sides

Chapter 10 Desserts

INTRODUCTION

As someone who loves to cook, I am always looking for ways to make food that is healthier and still tastes great. That is why I'm excited to introduce the Ninja Air Fryer Cookbook. The Ninja Air Fryer is a revolutionary kitchen appliance that is becoming increasingly popular due to its convenience and versatility.

I'm so excited to have found the Ninja Air Fryer! I'm looking forward to making healthier versions of all my favourite fried foods without compromising on taste. I'm sure that this air fryer will become a staple in my kitchen and that I will enjoy using it for years to come.

With this device, I can easily prepare various delicious meals quickly and with little to no oil. Since the Ninja Air Fryer is versatile, I can make all kinds of meals - from healthy snacks to full-fledged dinners. The recipes in this cookbook provide a wide variety of dishes to choose from, so I will never get bored.

Experience the ultimate in-home cooking with Ninja Air Fryer. This powerful, multi-functional appliance gives me the convenience and control to prepare my favourite meals quickly and easily. With its powerful heating element, I can enjoy crispy, golden-brown results without the extra oil and fat. Plus, the extra-large capacity allows me to create delicious meals for the whole family. Enjoy healthier, guilt-free cooking with Ninja Air Fryer.

Discover the world of healthier eating with the Ninja Air Fryer cookbook! This comprehensive guide is full of delicious recipes that are perfect for every occasion and budget. With a wide variety of recipes and easy-to-get ingredients, I'll be able to whip up tasty, healthy meals in no time. From snacks to entrees, there's something for everyone.

All of the recipes in this cookbook are cooked in the air fryer, so I can enjoy them guilt-free. With the Ninja Air Fryer cookbook, I can experience the joys of home-cooked meals without all the unhealthy oil and grease. This cookbook offers an exciting way to explore healthier eating and make nutritious meals for myself and my family.

The recipes designed in this cookbook are easy to follow, with simple ingredients and instructions. I will be able to make delicious meals in a short time, and I can also experiment with my unique cooking styles.

I can create something delicious with various flavours, textures, and colours. I am confident that this cookbook will provide us with countless delicious meals; we can enjoy with our family, friends, and loved ones.

Chapter 1 Ninja Air Fryer Basic Guide

Chapter 1 Ninja Air Fryer Basic Guide

The Ninja Air Fryer is a revolutionary kitchen appliance that makes delicious, healthy meals easy to cook in no time. It combines powerful air frying technology with a unique cyclonic grilling system to cook food with little to no oil. Making several delicious recipes with Ninja Air Fryer is a no-brainer.

With four preset cooking functions, the Ninja Air Fryer can cook a wide range of foods like fries, wings, and desserts. It also features a built-in digital timer and adjustable temperature control to ensure food cooking to perfection. With its sophisticated design and intuitive controls, the Ninja Air Fryer is the perfect addition to any kitchen.

The Ninja Air Fryer is a revolutionary kitchen appliance that uses rapid air technology to cook food with little or no oil. It works by circulating hot air around the food, which creates a crisp, golden-brown finish.

The air fryer also includes a removable basket to hold the food and a fan to circulate the hot air. The Ninja Air Fryer operates on two different settings.

The first setting is a high-temperature setting used to cook food quickly and efficiently. This setting is ideal for frozen foods such as French fries or chicken nuggets.

The second setting is a low-temperature setting for more delicate foods, such as fish or vegetables.

To use the Ninja Air Fryer, users must first set the temperature according to the type of food they are cooking. Once you set the temperature, place the food in the basket. Place the basket in the unit and close the lid. The Ninja Air Fryer then circulates hot air around the food to create a crispy and golden-brown finish.

The Ninja Air Fryer is a great way to cook food without adding extra calories to oil. It is also much faster than traditional deep-frying methods and requires little to no cleanup.

5 Features of Ninja Air Fryer

The Ninja Air Fryer is a revolutionary kitchen appliance quickly gaining popularity among health-conscious cooks. It uses rapid air technology to cook food with little to no oil, resulting in healthier and tastier meals. Here are five features that make the Ninja Air Fryer stand out from other air fryers.

Large Capacity

The Ninja Air Fryer has a 4-quart capacity, allowing you to cook large batches of food at once. It is perfect for large families or entertaining guests. The air fryer can hold up to 8 cups of food at once, giving you the ability to make a variety of dishes.

Easy to Clean

The Ninja Air Fryer has a non-stick cooking basket that is easy to clean. You can wipe it down with a damp cloth after each use, and you're ready to go. Its non-stick metal surface and detachable parts make wiping down and washing away any messes a simple task. The Ninja Air Fryer also has an oil-reducing feature that helps to reduce the amount of oil used while cooking.

Digital Interface

The Ninja Air Fryer has a digital interface that is easy to use. With just a few taps, you can select your desired cooking temperature, time, and food type.

Versatile Cooking

The Ninja Air Fryer cooks several kinds of food, from French fries and chicken wings to desserts like cakes and pies. The air fryer allows you to fry, bake, roast, and dehydrate foods with advanced air-frying technology. The air fryer quickly circulates hot air around the food, creating a crunchy, golden-brown exterior while keeping the inside juicy and tender. You can make all your favourite fried foods without the added fat and calories.

Healthy Eating

The Ninja Air Fryer uses little to no oil when cooking, resulting in healthier meals. Treating yourself to delicious meals without sacrificing your health is easy with the Ninja Air Fryer. It uses very little oil compared to traditional deep-frying but still gives you delicious, crunchy, and golden air-fried foods. Ninja Air Fryer allows you to make healthier versions of your favourite fried meals, like French fries, chicken wings, and many more.

Ninja Air Fryer Cooking Tips

Preheat Your Air Fryer

Preheating your air fryer before cooking is essential for the best cooking results. Preheating will help ensure that the temperature inside the air fryer is at the correct level for the food you are cooking.

Season Your Food

For the best flavour, season your food before you put it in the air fryer. Use a light seasoning such as salt, pepper, garlic powder, or other spices and herbs.

Use Oil Sparingly

Air fryers use very little oil. You can save big on oil expenses. A light spray of cooking oil will help ensure even cooking and prevent sticking.

Use Parchment Paper

To prevent sticking, place the food you are cooking on parchment paper or aluminium foil. It will also help keep your air fryer clean.
Don't Overcrowd the Air Fryer
Leave enough room in the air fryer for the food to cook evenly. Overcrowding can cause the food to steam instead of cook.

Shake the Basket

Shaking the basket will help ensure even cooking. It also helps to prevent food from sticking to the sides of the basket. Additionally, shaking the basket helps to circulate the hot air within the fryer speeding the cooking process.

Place Food in a Single Layer

Always place food in a single layer in the air fryer basket. Crowding the basket with food can prevent it from cooking evenly.

Keep a Close Eye

Keep a close eye on food when cooking and adjust the temperature or time as needed.

Use Fine Mist of Cooking Spray

You can prevent splattering by always using a fine mist of cooking spray on the basket before adding food.

Use Cooking Spray

When reheating food, spray the basket with cooking spray before adding the food.

Thaw Frozen Food

If cooking frozen food, it is best to thaw it first.

Add Butter for Taste

Add a small amount of oil or butter to the food to enhance the flavour and crispiness.

Use a Cookbook

Invest in an air fryer cookbook or look online for specific recipes and tips.

Pre-cook Food

If cooking large or thick pieces of food, consider pre-cooking them in the microwave first.

Use Dry Food

For best results, you can pat food dry with a paper towel before adding it to the air fryer.

Care and Cleaning

The Ninja Air Fryer is a great kitchen appliance for making tasty, healthy, and crunchy meals. You can ensure Ninja Air Fryer's proper working for years. It's essential to take care of it. Here are some tips on properly caring for and cleaning your Ninja Air Fryer.

1. Before and after each use, unplug your air fryer. It will help prevent electric shock and keep the appliance from malfunctioning.

2. Clean your air fryer's basket and pan with warm, soapy water after each use. If you're using the air fryer for multiple batches of food, it's best to wipe out the basket and pan with a damp cloth before adding more food.

3. Make sure to clean the interior and exterior of the air fryer regularly with a soft cloth and mild detergent. Do not use abrasive or harsh cleaning materials, such as steel wool or scouring pads, as these can damage the surface or cause scratches.

4. To remove any grease or oil buildup, make a paste of baking soda with water and use it to scrub the interior of the air fryer.

Cleaning and caring for your Ninja Air Fryer is easy! Make sure to empty and clean the basket and drawer after each use. Wipe down the exterior with a damp cloth and mild soap, and be sure to unplug the fryer before cleaning. With regular maintenance and proper care, your Ninja Air Fryer should give you years of delicious cooking!

Chapter 2 Holiday Specials

Chapter 2 Holiday Specials

Teriyaki Shrimp Skewers

Prep time: 10 minutes | Cook time: 6 minutes |
Makes 12 skewered shrimp

1½ tablespoons mirin
1½ teaspoons ginger paste
1½ tablespoons soy sauce
12 large shrimp, peeled and

deveined
1 large egg
180 ml panko breadcrumbs
Cooking spray

Combine the mirin, ginger paste, and soy sauce in a large bowl. Stir to mix well. Dunk the shrimp in the bowl of mirin mixture, then wrap the bowl in plastic and refrigerate for 1 hour to marinate. Preheat the air fryer to 200ºC. Spritz the air fryer basket with cooking spray. Run twelve 4-inch skewers through each shrimp. Whisk the egg in the bowl of marinade to combine well. Pour the breadcrumbs on a plate. Dredge the shrimp skewers in the egg mixture, then shake the excess off and roll over the breadcrumbs to coat well. Arrange the shrimp skewers in the preheated air fryer and spritz with cooking spray. You need to work in batches to avoid overcrowding. Air fry for 6 minutes or until the shrimp are opaque and firm. Flip the shrimp skewers halfway through. Serve immediately.

Crispy Green Tomato Slices

Prep time: 10 minutes | Cook time: 8 minutes |
Makes 12 slices

120 ml plain flour
1 egg
120 ml buttermilk
235 ml cornmeal
235 ml panko breadcrumbs
2 green tomatoes, cut into

¼-inch-thick slices, patted dry
½ teaspoon salt
½ teaspoon ground black
pepper
Cooking spray

Preheat the air fryer to 200ºC. Line the air fryer basket with parchment paper. Pour the flour in a bowl. Whisk the egg and buttermilk in a second bowl. Combine the cornmeal and panko breadcrumbs in a third bowl. Dredge the tomato slices in the bowl of flour first, then into the egg mixture, and then dunk the slices into the cornmeal mixture. Shake the excess off. Transfer the well-coated tomato slices in the preheated air fryer and sprinkle with salt and ground black pepper. Spritz the tomato slices with cooking spray. Air fry for 8 minutes or until crispy and lightly browned. Flip the slices halfway through the cooking time. Serve immediately.

Simple Baked Green Beans

Prep time: 5 minutes | Cook time: 10 minutes |
Makes 475 ml

½ teaspoon lemon pepper
2 teaspoons granulated garlic
½ teaspoon salt

1 tablespoon olive oil
475 ml fresh green beans,
trimmed and snapped in half

Preheat the air fryer to 190ºC. Combine the lemon pepper, garlic, salt, and olive oil in a bowl. Stir to mix well. Add the green beans to the bowl of mixture and toss to coat well. Arrange the green beans in the preheated air fryer. Bake for 10 minutes or until tender and crispy. Shake the basket halfway through to make sure the green beans are cooked evenly. Serve immediately.

Garlicky Olive Stromboli

Prep time: 25 minutes | Cook time: 25 minutes | Serves 8

4 large cloves garlic, unpeeled
3 tablespoons grated Parmesan
cheese
120 ml packed fresh basil
leaves
120 ml marinated, pitted green
and black olives

¼ teaspoon crushed red pepper
230 g pizza dough, at room
temperature
110 g sliced provolone cheese
(about 8 slices)
Cooking spray

Preheat the air fryer to 190ºC. Spritz the air fryer basket with cooking spray. Put the unpeeled garlic in the air fryer basket. Air fry for 10 minutes or until the garlic is softened completely. Remove them from the air fryer and allow to cool until you can handle. Peel the garlic and place into a food processor with 2 tablespoons of Parmesan, basil, olives, and crushed red pepper. Pulse to mix well. Set aside. Arrange the pizza dough on a clean work surface, then roll it out with a rolling pin into a rectangle. Cut the rectangle in half. Sprinkle half of the garlic mixture over each rectangle half and leave ½-inch edges uncover. Top them with the provolone cheese. Brush one long side of each rectangle half with water, then roll them up. Spritz the air fryer basket with cooking spray. Transfer the rolls in the preheated air fryer. Spritz with cooking spray and scatter with remaining Parmesan. Air fry the rolls for 15 minutes or until golden brown. Flip the rolls halfway through. Remove the rolls from the air fryer and allow to cool for a few minutes before serving.

Classic Churros

Prep time: 35 minutes | Cook time: 10 minutes per batch | Makes 12 churros

4 tablespoons butter	2 large eggs
¼ teaspoon salt	2 teaspoons ground cinnamon
120 ml water	60 ml granulated white sugar
120 ml plain flour	Cooking spray

Put the butter, salt, and water in a saucepan. Bring to a boil until the butter is melted on high heat. Keep stirring. Reduce the heat to medium and fold in the flour to form a dough. Keep cooking and stirring until the dough is dried out and coat the pan with a crust. Turn off the heat and scrape the dough in a large bowl. Allow to cool for 15 minutes. Break and whisk the eggs into the dough with a hand mixer until the dough is sanity and firm enough to shape. Scoop up 1 tablespoon of the dough and roll it into a ½-inch-diameter and 2-inch-long cylinder. Repeat with remaining dough to make 12 cylinders in total. Combine the cinnamon and sugar in a large bowl and dunk the cylinders into the cinnamon mix to coat. Arrange the cylinders on a plate and refrigerate for 20 minutes. Preheat the air fryer to 190ºC. Spritz the air fryer basket with cooking spray. Place the cylinders in batches in the air fryer basket and spritz with cooking spray. Air fry for 10 minutes or until golden brown and fluffy. Flip them halfway through. Serve immediately.

South Carolina Shrimp and Corn Bake

Prep time: 10 minutes | Cook time: 18 minutes | Serves 2

1 ear corn, husk and silk removed, cut into 2-inch rounds	pepper
227 g red potatoes, unpeeled, cut into 1-inch pieces	227 g large shrimps (about 12 shrimps), deveined
2 teaspoons Old Bay or all-purpose seasoning, divided	170 g andouille or chorizo sausage, cut into 1-inch pieces
2 teaspoons vegetable oil, divided	2 garlic cloves, minced
¼ teaspoon ground black	1 tablespoon chopped fresh parsley

Preheat the air fryer to 200ºC. Put the corn rounds and potatoes in a large bowl. Sprinkle with 1 teaspoon of seasoning and drizzle with vegetable oil. Toss to coat well. Transfer the corn rounds and potatoes on a baking sheet, then put in the preheated air fryer. Bake for 12 minutes or until soft and browned. Shake the basket halfway through the cooking time. Meanwhile, cut slits into the shrimps but be careful not to cut them through. Combine the shrimps, sausage, remaining seasoning, and remaining vegetable oil in the large bowl. Toss to coat well. When the baking of the potatoes and corn rounds is complete, add the shrimps and sausage and bake for 6 more minutes or until the shrimps are opaque. Shake the basket halfway through the cooking time. When the baking is finished, serve them on a plate and spread with parsley before serving.

Cinnamon Rolls with Cream Glaze

Prep time: 2 hours 15 minutes | Cook time: 10 minutes | Serves 8

450 g frozen bread dough, thawed	Cream Glaze:
2 tablespoons melted butter	110 g soft white cheese
1½ tablespoons cinnamon	½ teaspoon vanilla extract
180 ml brown sugar	2 tablespoons melted butter
Cooking spray	300 ml powdered erythritol

Place the bread dough on a clean work surface, then roll the dough out into a rectangle with a rolling pin. Brush the top of the dough with melted butter and leave 1-inch edges uncovered. Combine the cinnamon and sugar in a small bowl, then sprinkle the dough with the cinnamon mixture. Roll the dough over tightly, then cut the dough log into 8 portions. Wrap the portions in plastic, better separately, and let sit to rise for 1 or 2 hours. Meanwhile, combine the ingredients for the glaze in a separate small bowl. Stir to mix well. Preheat the air fryer to 175ºC. Spritz the air fryer basket with cooking spray. Transfer the risen rolls to the preheated air fryer. You may need to work in batches to avoid overcrowding. Air fry for 5 minutes or until golden brown. Flip the rolls halfway through. Serve the rolls with the glaze.

Whole Chicken Roast

Prep time: 10 minutes | Cook time: 1 hour | Serves 6

1 teaspoon salt	½ teaspoon garlic powder
1 teaspoon Italian seasoning	½ teaspoon onion powder
½ teaspoon freshly ground black pepper	2 tablespoons olive oil, plus more as needed
½ teaspoon paprika	1 (1.8 kg) small chicken

Preheat the air fryer to 180ºC. Grease the air fryer basket lightly with olive oil. In a small bowl, mix the salt, Italian seasoning, pepper, paprika, garlic powder, and onion powder. Remove any giblets from the chicken. Pat the chicken dry thoroughly with paper towels, including the cavity. Brush the chicken all over with the olive oil and rub it with the seasoning mixture. Truss the chicken or tie the legs with butcher's twine. This will make it easier to flip the chicken during cooking. Put the chicken in the air fryer basket, breast-side down. Air fry for 30 minutes. Flip the chicken over and baste it with any drippings collected in the bottom drawer of the air fryer. Lightly brush the chicken with olive oil. Air fry for 20 minutes. Flip the chicken over one last time and air fry until a thermometer inserted into the thickest part of the thigh reaches at least 75ºC and it's crispy and golden, 10 more minutes. Continue to cook, checking every 5 minutes until the chicken reaches the correct internal temperature. Let the chicken rest for 10 minutes before carving and serving.

Simple Air Fried Crispy Brussels Sprouts

Prep time: 5 minutes | Cook time: 20 minutes | Serves 4

¼ teaspoon salt	oil
⅛ teaspoon ground black pepper	450 g Brussels sprouts, trimmed and halved
1 tablespoon extra-virgin olive	Lemon wedges, for garnish

Preheat the air fryer to 175ºC. Combine the salt, black pepper, and olive oil in a large bowl. Stir to mix well. Add the Brussels sprouts to the bowl of mixture and toss to coat well. Arrange the Brussels sprouts in the preheated air fryer. Air fry for 20 minutes or until lightly browned and wilted. Shake the basket two times during the air frying. Transfer the cooked Brussels sprouts to a large plate and squeeze the lemon wedges on top to serve.

Hearty Honey Yeast Rolls

**Prep time: 10 minutes | Cook time: 20 minutes |
Makes 8 rolls**

60 ml whole milk, heated to 45ºC in the microwave	½ teaspoon rock salt
½ teaspoon active dry yeast	2 tablespoons unsalted butter, at room temperature, plus more for greasing
1 tablespoon honey	
160 ml plain flour, plus more for dusting	Flaky sea salt, to taste

In a large bowl, whisk together the milk, yeast, and honey and let stand until foamy, about 10 minutes. Stir in the flour and salt until just combined. Stir in the butter until absorbed. Scrape the dough onto a lightly floured work surface and knead until smooth, about 6 minutes. Transfer the dough to a lightly greased bowl, cover loosely with a sheet of plastic wrap or a kitchen towel, and let sit until nearly doubled in size, about 1 hour. Uncover the dough, lightly press it down to expel the bubbles, then portion it into 8 equal pieces. Prep the work surface by wiping it clean with a damp paper towel (if there is flour on the work surface, it will prevent the dough from sticking lightly to the surface, which helps it form a ball). Roll each piece into a ball by cupping the palm of the hand around the dough against the work surface and moving the heel of the hand in a circular motion while using the thumb to contain the dough and tighten it into a perfectly round ball. Once all the balls are formed, nestle them side by side in the air fryer basket. Cover the rolls loosely with a kitchen towel or a sheet of plastic wrap and let sit until lightly risen and puffed, 20 to 30 minutes. Preheat the air fryer to 130ºC. Uncover the rolls and gently brush with more butter, being careful not to press the rolls too hard. Air fry until the rolls are light golden brown and fluffy, about 12 minutes. Remove the rolls from the air fryer and brush liberally with more butter, if you like, and sprinkle each roll with a pinch of sea salt. Serve warm.

Simple Cheesy Shrimps

**Prep time: 10 minutes | Cook time: 16 minutes |
Serves 4 to 6**

160 ml grated Parmesan cheese	2 tablespoons olive oil
4 minced garlic cloves	900 g cooked large shrimps, peeled and deveined
1 teaspoon onion powder	
½ teaspoon oregano	Lemon wedges, for topping
1 teaspoon basil	Cooking spray
1 teaspoon ground black pepper	

Preheat the air fryer to 175ºC. Spritz the air fryer basket with cooking spray. Combine all the ingredients, except for the shrimps, in a large bowl. Stir to mix well. Dunk the shrimps in the mixture and toss to coat well. Shake the excess off. Arrange the shrimps in the preheated air fryer. Air fry for 8 minutes or until opaque. Flip the shrimps halfway through. You may need to work in batches to avoid overcrowding. Transfer the cooked shrimps on a large plate and squeeze the lemon wedges over before serving.

Shrimp with Sriracha and Worcestershire Sauce

**Prep time: 15 minutes | Cook time: 10 minutes per
batch | Serves 4**

1 tablespoon Sriracha sauce	235 ml panko breadcrumbs
1 teaspoon Worcestershire sauce	450 g raw shrimp, shelled and deveined, rinsed and drained
2 tablespoons sweet chilli sauce	Lime wedges, for serving
180 ml mayonnaise	Cooking spray
1 egg, beaten	

Preheat the air fryer to 180ºC. Spritz the air fryer basket with cooking spray. Combine the Sriracha sauce, Worcestershire sauce, chilli sauce, and mayo in a bowl. Stir to mix well. Reserve 80 ml the mixture as the dipping sauce. Combine the remaining sauce mixture with the beaten egg. Stir to mix well. Put the panko in a separate bowl. Dredge the shrimp in the sauce mixture first, then into the panko. Roll the shrimp to coat well. Shake the excess off. Place the shrimp in the preheated air fryer, then spritz with cooking spray. You may need to work in batches to avoid overcrowding. Air fry the shrimp for 10 minutes or until opaque. Flip the shrimp halfway through the cooking time. Remove the shrimp from the air fryer and serve with reserve sauce mixture and squeeze the lime wedges over.

Hasselback Potatoes

Prep time: 5 minutes | Cook time: 50 minutes | Serves 4

4 russet or Maris Piper potatoes, peeled
Salt and freshly ground black pepper, to taste

60 ml grated Parmesan cheese
Cooking spray

Preheat the air fryer to 200°C. Spray the air fryer basket lightly with cooking spray. Make thin parallel cuts into each potato, ⅛-inch to ¼-inch apart, stopping at about ½ of the way through. The potato needs to stay intact along the bottom. Spray the potatoes with cooking spray and use the hands or a silicone brush to completely coat the potatoes lightly in oil. Put the potatoes, sliced side up, in the air fryer basket in a single layer. Leave a little room between each potato. Sprinkle the potatoes lightly with salt and black pepper. Air fry for 20 minutes. Reposition the potatoes and spritz lightly with cooking spray again. Air fry until the potatoes are fork-tender and crispy and browned, another 20 to 30 minutes. Sprinkle the potatoes with Parmesan cheese and serve.

Lemony and Garlicky Asparagus

Prep time: 5 minutes | Cook time: 10 minutes | Makes 10 spears

10 spears asparagus (about 230 g in total), snap the ends off
1 tablespoon lemon juice
2 teaspoons minced garlic

½ teaspoon salt
¼ teaspoon ground black pepper
Cooking spray

Preheat the air fryer to 200°C. Line a parchment paper in the air fryer basket. Put the asparagus spears in a large bowl. Drizzle with lemon juice and sprinkle with minced garlic, salt, and ground black pepper. Toss to coat well. Transfer the asparagus in the preheated air fryer and spritz with cooking spray. Air fryer for 10 minutes or until wilted and soft. Flip the asparagus halfway through. Serve immediately.

Chapter 3 Snacks and Appetisers

Chapter 3 Snacks and Appetisers

Chilli-Brined Fried Calamari

Prep time: 20 minutes | Cook time: 8 minutes | Serves 2

1 (227 g) jar sweet or hot pickled cherry peppers	black pepper, to taste
227 g calamari bodies and tentacles, bodies cut into ½-inch-wide rings	3 large eggs, lightly beaten
	Cooking spray
	120 ml mayonnaise
1 lemon	1 teaspoon finely chopped rosemary
475 ml plain flour	
Rock salt and freshly ground	1 garlic clove, minced

1. Drain the pickled pepper brine into a large bowl and tear the peppers into bite-size strips. Add the pepper strips and calamari to the brine and let stand in the refrigerator for 20 minutes or up to 2 hours. 2. Grate the lemon zest into a large bowl then whisk in the flour and season with salt and pepper. Dip the calamari and pepper strips in the egg, then toss them in the flour mixture until fully coated. Spray the calamari and peppers liberally with cooking spray, then transfer half to the air fryer. Air fry at 200ºC, shaking the basket halfway into cooking, until the calamari is cooked through and golden brown, about 8 minutes. Transfer to a plate and repeat with the remaining pieces. 3. In a small bowl, whisk together the mayonnaise, rosemary, and garlic. Squeeze half the zested lemon to get 1 tablespoon of juice and stir it into the sauce. Season with salt and pepper. Cut the remaining zested lemon half into 4 small wedges and serve alongside the calamari, peppers, and sauce.

Garlic-Roasted Tomatoes and Olives

Prep time: 5 minutes | Cook time: 20 minutes | Serves 6

475 ml cherry tomatoes	1 tablespoon fresh basil, minced
4 garlic cloves, roughly chopped	1 tablespoon fresh oregano, minced
½ red onion, roughly chopped	2 tablespoons olive oil
240 ml black olives	¼ to ½ teaspoon salt
240 ml green olives	

1. Preheat the air fryer to 190ºC. 2. In a large bowl, combine all of the ingredients and toss together so that the tomatoes and olives are coated well with the olive oil and herbs. 3. Pour the mixture into the air fryer basket, and roast for 10 minutes. Stir the mixture well, then continue roasting for an additional 10 minutes. 4. Remove from the air fryer, transfer to a serving bowl, and enjoy.

Sweet Potato Fries with Mayonnaise

Prep time: 5 minutes | Cook time: 20 minutes |
Serves 2 to 3

1 large sweet potato (about 450 g), scrubbed	60 ml light mayonnaise
	½ teaspoon sriracha sauce
1 teaspoon vegetable or rapeseed oil	1 tablespoon spicy brown mustard
Salt, to taste	1 tablespoon sweet Thai chilli sauce
Dipping Sauce:	

1. Preheat the air fryer to 90ºC. 2. On a flat work surface, cut the sweet potato into fry-shaped strips about ¼ inch wide and ¼ inch thick. You can use a mandoline to slice the sweet potato quickly and uniformly. 3. In a medium bowl, drizzle the sweet potato strips with the oil and toss well. 4. Transfer to the air fryer basket and air fry for 10 minutes, shaking the basket twice during cooking. 5. Remove the air fryer basket and sprinkle with the salt and toss to coat. 6. Increase the air fryer temperature to 200ºC and air fry for an additional 10 minutes, or until the fries are crispy and tender. Shake the basket a few times during cooking. 7. Meanwhile, whisk together all the ingredients for the sauce in a small bowl. 8. Remove the sweet potato fries from the basket to a plate and serve warm alongside the dipping sauce.

Tangy Fried Pickle Spears

Prep time: 5 minutes | Cook time: 15 minutes | Serves 6

2 jars sweet and sour pickle spears, patted dry	1 teaspoon sea salt
	½ teaspoon shallot powder
2 medium-sized eggs	⅓ teaspoon chilli powder
80 ml milk	80 ml plain flour
1 teaspoon garlic powder	Cooking spray

1. Preheat the air fryer to 195ºC. Spritz the air fryer basket with cooking spray. 2. In a bowl, beat together the eggs with milk. In another bowl, combine garlic powder, sea salt, shallot powder, chilli powder and plain flour until well blended. 3. One by one, roll the pickle spears in the powder mixture, then dredge them in the egg mixture. Dip them in the powder mixture a second time for additional coating. 4. Arrange the coated pickles in the prepared basket. Air fry for 15 minutes until golden and crispy, shaking the basket halfway through to ensure even cooking. 5. Transfer to a plate and let cool for 5 minutes before serving.

Crunchy Basil White Beans

Prep time: 2 minutes | Cook time: 19 minutes | Serves 2

1 (425 g) can cooked white
beans
2 tablespoons olive oil
1 teaspoon fresh sage, chopped

¼ teaspoon garlic powder
¼ teaspoon salt, divided
1 teaspoon chopped fresh basil

1. Preheat the air fryer to 190ºC. 2. In a medium bowl, mix together the beans, olive oil, sage, garlic, ⅛ teaspoon salt, and basil. 3. Pour the white beans into the air fryer and spread them out in a single layer. 4. Bake for 10 minutes. Stir and continue cooking for an additional 5 to 9 minutes, or until they reach your preferred level of crispiness. 5. Toss with the remaining ⅛ teaspoon salt before serving.

Lemony Pear Chips

Prep time: 15 minutes | Cook time: 9 to 13 minutes | Serves 4

2 firm Bosc or Anjou pears, cut
crosswise into ⅛-inch-thick
slices
1 tablespoon freshly squeezed

lemon juice
½ teaspoon ground cinnamon
⅛ teaspoon ground cardamom

1. Preheat the air fryer to 190ºC. 2. Separate the smaller stem-end pear rounds from the larger rounds with seeds. Remove the core and seeds from the larger slices. Sprinkle all slices with lemon juice, cinnamon, and cardamom. 3. Put the smaller chips into the air fryer basket. Air fry for 3 to 5 minutes, or until light golden brown, shaking the basket once during cooking. Remove from the air fryer. 4. Repeat with the larger slices, air frying for 6 to 8 minutes, or until light golden brown, shaking the basket once during cooking. 5. Remove the chips from the air fryer. Cool and serve or store in an airtight container at room temperature up for to 2 days.

Classic Spring Rolls

Prep time: 10 minutes | Cook time: 9 minutes | Makes 16 spring rolls

4 teaspoons toasted sesame oil
6 medium garlic cloves, minced
or pressed
1 tablespoon grated peeled
fresh ginger
475 ml thinly sliced shiitake
mushrooms
1 L chopped green cabbage

240 ml grated carrot
½ teaspoon sea salt
16 rice paper wrappers
Cooking oil spray (sunflower,
safflower, or refined coconut)
Gluten-free sweet and sour
sauce or Thai sweet chilli sauce,
for serving (optional)

1. Place a wok or sauté pan over medium heat until hot. 2. Add the sesame oil, garlic, ginger, mushrooms, cabbage, carrot, and salt. Cook for 3 to 4 minutes, stirring often, until the cabbage is lightly wilted. Remove the pan from the heat. 3. Gently run a rice paper under water. Lay it on a flat non-absorbent surface. Place about 60 ml of the cabbage filling in the middle. Once the wrapper is soft enough to roll, fold the bottom up over the filling, fold in the sides, and roll the wrapper all the way up. (Basically, make a tiny burrito.) 4. Repeat step 3 to make the remaining spring rolls until you have the number of spring rolls you want to cook right now (and the amount that will fit in the air fryer basket in a single layer without them touching each other). Refrigerate any leftover filling in an airtight container for about 1 week. 5. Insert the crisper plate into the basket and the basket into the unit. Preheat the unit by selecting AIR FRY, setting the temperature to 200ºC, and setting the time to 3 minutes. Select START/STOP to begin. 6. Once the unit is preheated, spray the crisper plate and the basket with cooking oil. Place the spring rolls into the basket, leaving a little room between them so they don't stick to each other. Spray the top of each spring roll with cooking oil. 7. Select AIR FRY, set the temperature to 200ºC, and set the time to 9 minutes. Select START/STOP to begin. 8. When the cooking is complete, the egg rolls should be crisp-ish and lightly browned. Serve immediately, plain or with a sauce of choice.

Pepperoni Pizza Dip

Prep time: 10 minutes | Cook time: 10 minutes | Serves 6

170 g soft white cheese
177 ml shredded Italian cheese
blend
60 ml sour cream
1½ teaspoons dried Italian
seasoning
¼ teaspoon garlic salt
¼ teaspoon onion powder
177 ml pizza sauce

120 ml sliced miniature
pepperoni
60 ml sliced black olives
1 tablespoon thinly sliced green
onion
Cut-up raw vegetables, toasted
baguette slices, pitta chips, or
tortilla chips, for serving

1. In a small bowl, combine the soft white cheese, 60 ml of the shredded cheese, the sour cream, Italian seasoning, garlic salt, and onion powder. Stir until smooth and the ingredients are well blended. 2. Spread the mixture in a baking pan. Top with the pizza sauce, spreading to the edges. Sprinkle with the remaining 120 ml shredded cheese. Arrange the pepperoni slices on top of the cheese. Top with the black olives and green onion. 3. Place the pan in the air fryer basket. Set the air fryer to 175ºC for 10 minutes, or until the pepperoni is beginning to brown on the edges and the cheese is bubbly and lightly browned. 4. Let stand for 5 minutes before serving with vegetables, toasted baguette slices, pitta chips, or tortilla chips.

Roasted Pearl Onion Dip

Prep time: 5 minutes | Cook time: 12 minutes | Serves 4

475 ml peeled pearl onions	1 tablespoon lemon juice
3 garlic cloves	¼ teaspoon black pepper
3 tablespoons olive oil, divided	⅛ teaspoon red pepper flakes
½ teaspoon salt	Pitta chips, vegetables, or
240 ml non-fat plain Greek yoghurt	toasted bread for serving (optional)

1. Preheat the air fryer to 180°C. 2. In a large bowl, combine the pearl onions and garlic with 2 tablespoons of the olive oil until the onions are well coated. 3. Pour the garlic-and-onion mixture into the air fryer basket and roast for 12 minutes. 4. Transfer the garlic and onions to a food processor. Pulse the vegetables several times, until the onions are minced but still have some chunks. 5. In a large bowl, combine the garlic and onions and the remaining 1 tablespoon of olive oil, along with the salt, yoghurt, lemon juice, black pepper, and red pepper flakes. 6. Cover and chill for 1 hour before serving with pitta chips, vegetables, or toasted bread.

Golden Onion Rings

Prep time: 15 minutes | Cook time: 14 minutes per batch | Serves 4

1 large white onion, peeled and cut into ½ to ¾-inch-thick slices (about 475 ml)	black pepper, divided
	¾ teaspoon granulated garlic, divided
120 ml semi-skimmed milk	355 ml wholemeal
240 ml wholemeal pastry flour, or plain flour	breadcrumbs, or gluten-free breadcrumbs
2 tablespoons cornflour	Cooking oil spray (coconut,
¾ teaspoon sea salt, divided	sunflower, or safflower)
½ teaspoon freshly ground	Ketchup, for serving (optional)

1. Carefully separate the onion slices into rings—a gentle touch is important here. 2. Place the milk in a shallow bowl and set aside. 3. Make the first breading: In a medium bowl, stir together the flour, cornflour, ¼ teaspoon of salt, ¼ teaspoon of pepper, and ¼ teaspoon of granulated garlic. Set aside. 4. Make the second breading: In a separate medium bowl, stir together the breadcrumbs with the remaining ½ teaspoon of salt, the remaining ½ teaspoon of garlic, and the remaining ½ teaspoon of pepper. Set aside. 5. Insert the crisper plate into the basket and the basket into the unit. Preheat the unit by selecting AIR FRY, setting the temperature to 200°C, and setting the time to 3 minutes. Select START/STOP to begin. 6. Once the unit is preheated, spray the crisper plate and the basket with cooking oil. 7. To make the onion rings, dip one ring into the milk and into the first breading mixture. Dip the ring into the milk again and back into the first breading mixture, coating thoroughly. Dip the ring into the milk one last time and then into the second breading mixture, coating thoroughly. Gently lay the onion ring in the basket. Repeat with additional rings and, as you place them into the basket, do not overlap them too much. Once all the onion rings are in the basket, generously spray the tops with cooking oil. 8. Select AIR FRY, set the temperature to 200°C, and set the time to 14 minutes. Insert the basket into the unit. Select START/STOP to begin. 9. After 4 minutes, open the unit and spray the rings generously with cooking oil. Close the unit to resume cooking. After 3 minutes, remove the basket and spray the onion rings again. Remove the rings, turn them over, and place them back into the basket. Generously spray them again with oil. Reinsert the basket to resume cooking. After 4 minutes, generously spray the rings with oil one last time. Resume cooking for the remaining 3 minutes, or until the onion rings are very crunchy and brown. 10. When the cooking is complete, serve the hot rings with ketchup, or other sauce of choice.

Garlic-Parmesan Croutons

Prep time: 3 minutes | Cook time: 12 minutes | Serves 4

Oil, for spraying	3 tablespoons olive oil
1 L cubed French bread	1 tablespoon granulated garlic
1 tablespoon grated Parmesan cheese	½ teaspoon unsalted salt

1. Line the air fryer basket with parchment and spray lightly with oil. 2. In a large bowl, mix together the bread, Parmesan cheese, olive oil, garlic, and salt, tossing with your hands to evenly distribute the seasonings. Transfer the coated bread cubes to the prepared basket. 3. Air fry at 175°C for 10 to 12 minutes, stirring once after 5 minutes, or until crisp and golden brown.

Bacon-Wrapped Shrimp and Jalapeño

Prep time: 20 minutes | Cook time: 26 minutes | Serves 8

24 large shrimp, peeled and deveined, about 340 g	divided
5 tablespoons barbecue sauce,	12 strips bacon, cut in half
	24 small pickled jalapeño slices

1. Toss together the shrimp and 3 tablespoons of the barbecue sauce. Let stand for 15 minutes. Soak 24 wooden toothpicks in water for 10 minutes. Wrap 1 piece bacon around the shrimp and jalapeño slice, then secure with a toothpick. 2. Preheat the air fryer to 175°C. 3. Working in batches, place half of the shrimp in the air fryer basket, spacing them ½ inch apart. Air fry for 10 minutes. Turn shrimp over with tongs and air fry for 3 minutes more, or until bacon is golden brown and shrimp are cooked through. 4. Brush with the remaining barbecue sauce and serve.

Skinny Fries

Prep time: 10 minutes | Cook time: 15 minutes per batch | Serves 2

2 to 3 russet or Maris Piper potatoes, peeled and cut into ¼-inch sticks
2 to 3 teaspoons olive or vegetable oil
Salt, to taste

1. Cut the potatoes into ¼-inch strips. (A mandolin with a julienne blade is really helpful here.) Rinse the potatoes with cold water several times and let them soak in cold water for at least 10 minutes or as long as overnight. 2. Preheat the air fryer to 190ºC. 3. Drain and dry the potato sticks really well, using a clean kitchen towel. Toss the fries with the oil in a bowl and then air fry the fries in two batches at 190ºC for 15 minutes, shaking the basket a couple of times while they cook. 4. Add the first batch of French fries back into the air fryer basket with the finishing batch and let everything warm through for a few minutes. As soon as the fries are done, season them with salt and transfer to a plate or basket. Serve them warm with ketchup or your favourite dip.

Jalapeño Poppers

Prep time: 10 minutes | Cook time: 20 minutes | Serves 4

Oil, for spraying
227 g soft white cheese
177 ml gluten-free breadcrumbs, divided
2 tablespoons chopped fresh parsley
½ teaspoon granulated garlic
½ teaspoon salt
10 jalapeño peppers, halved and seeded

1. Line the air fryer basket with parchment and spray lightly with oil. 2. In a medium bowl, mix together the soft white cheese, half of the breadcrumbs, the parsley, garlic, and salt. 3. Spoon the mixture into the jalapeño halves. Gently press the stuffed jalapeños in the remaining breadcrumbs. 4. Place the stuffed jalapeños in the prepared basket. 5. Air fry at 190ºC for 20 minutes, or until the cheese is melted and the breadcrumbs are crisp and golden brown.

Turkey Burger Sliders

Prep time: 10 minutes | Cook time: 5 to 7 minutes | Makes 8 sliders

450 g minced turkey
¼ teaspoon curry powder
1 teaspoon Hoisin sauce
½ teaspoon salt
8 slider rolls
120 ml slivered red onions
120 ml slivered green or red pepper
120 ml fresh chopped pineapple
Light soft white cheese

1. Combine turkey, curry powder, Hoisin sauce, and salt and mix together well. 2. Shape turkey mixture into 8 small patties. 3. Place patties in air fryer basket and air fry at 180ºC for 5 to 7 minutes, until patties are well done, and juices run clear. 4. Place each patty on the bottom half of a slider roll and top with onions, peppers, and pineapple. Spread the remaining bun halves with soft white cheese to taste, place on top, and serve.

Chapter 4 Breakfasts

Chapter 4 Breakfasts

Simple Cinnamon Toasts

Prep time: 5 minutes | Cook time: 4 minutes | Serves 4

1 tablespoon salted butter
2 teaspoons ground cinnamon
4 tablespoons sugar
½ teaspoon vanilla extract
10 bread slices

1. Preheat the air fryer to 190ºC. 2. In a bowl, combine the butter, cinnamon, sugar, and vanilla extract. Spread onto the slices of bread. 3. Put the bread inside the air fryer and bake for 4 minutes or until golden brown. 4. Serve warm.

Bacon and Spinach Egg Muffins

Prep time: 7 minutes | Cook time: 12 to 14 minutes | Serves 6

6 large eggs
60 ml double (whipping) cream
½ teaspoon sea salt
¼ teaspoon freshly ground black pepper
¼ teaspoon cayenne pepper
(optional)
180 ml frozen chopped spinach, thawed and drained
4 strips cooked bacon, crumbled
60 g shredded Cheddar cheese

1. In a large bowl (with a spout if you have one), whisk together the eggs, double cream, salt, black pepper, and cayenne pepper (if using). 2. Divide the spinach and bacon among 6 silicone muffin cups. Place the muffin cups in your air fryer basket. 3. Divide the egg mixture among the muffin cups. Top with the cheese. 4. Set the air fryer to 150ºC. Bake for 12 to 14 minutes, until the eggs are set and cooked through.

Turkey Breakfast Sausage Patties

Prep time: 5 minutes | Cook time: 10 minutes | Serves 4

1 tablespoon chopped fresh thyme
1 tablespoon chopped fresh sage
1¼ teaspoons coarse or flaky salt
1 teaspoon chopped fennel seeds
120 ml finely minced sweet apple (peeled)
¾ teaspoon smoked paprika
½ teaspoon onion granules
½ teaspoon garlic powder
⅛ teaspoon crushed red pepper flakes
⅛ teaspoon freshly ground black pepper
450 g lean turkey mince

1. Thoroughly combine the thyme, sage, salt, fennel seeds, paprika, onion granules, garlic powder, red pepper flakes, and black pepper in a medium bowl. 2. Add the turkey mince and apple and stir until well incorporated. Divide the mixture into 8 equal portions and shape into patties with your hands, each about ¼ inch thick and 3 inches in diameter. 3. Preheat the air fryer to 200ºC. 4. Place the patties in the air fryer basket in a single layer. You may need to work in batches to avoid overcrowding. 5. Air fry for 5 minutes. Flip the patties and air fry for 5 minutes, or until the patties are nicely browned and cooked through. 6. Remove from the basket to a plate and repeat with the remaining patties. 7. Serve warm.

Parmesan Sausage Egg Muffins

Prep time: 5 minutes | Cook time: 20 minutes | Serves 4

170 g Italian-seasoned sausage, sliced
6 eggs
30 ml double cream
Salt and ground black pepper, to taste
85 g Parmesan cheese, grated

1. Preheat the air fryer to 175ºC. Grease a muffin pan. 2. Put the sliced sausage in the muffin pan. 3. Beat the eggs with the cream in a bowl and season with salt and pepper. 4. Pour half of the mixture over the sausages in the pan. 5. Sprinkle with cheese and the remaining egg mixture. 6. Bake in the preheated air fryer for 20 minutes or until set. 7. Serve immediately.

Parmesan Ranch Risotto

Prep time: 10 minutes | Cook time: 30 minutes | Serves 2

1 tablespoon olive oil
1 clove garlic, minced
1 tablespoon unsalted butter
1 onion, diced
180 ml Arborio rice
475 ml chicken stock, boiling
120 ml Parmesan cheese, grated

1. Preheat the air fryer to 200ºC. 2. Grease a round baking tin with olive oil and stir in the garlic, butter, and onion. 3. Transfer the tin to the air fryer and bake for 4 minutes. Add the rice and bake for 4 more minutes. 4. Turn the air fryer to 160ºC and pour in the chicken stock. Cover and bake for 22 minutes. 5. Scatter with cheese and serve.

Cheddar-Ham-Corn Muffins

Prep time: 10 minutes | Cook time: 6 to 8 minutes per batch | Makes 8 muffins

180 ml cornmeal/polenta	120 ml shredded sharp Cheddar
60 ml flour	cheese
1½ teaspoons baking powder	120 ml diced ham
¼ teaspoon salt	8 foil muffin cups, liners
1 egg, beaten	removed and sprayed with
2 tablespoons rapeseed oil	cooking spray
120 ml milk	

1. Preheat the air fryer to 200°C. 2. In a medium bowl, stir together the cornmeal, flour, baking powder, and salt. 3. Add egg, oil, and milk to dry ingredients and mix well. 4. Stir in shredded cheese and diced ham. 5. Divide batter among the muffin cups. 6. Place 4 filled muffin cups in air fryer basket and bake for 5 minutes. 7. Reduce temperature to 165°C and bake for 1 to 2 minutes or until toothpick inserted in center of muffin comes out clean. 8. Repeat steps 6 and 7 to cook remaining muffins.

Sirloin Steaks with Eggs

Prep time: 8 minutes | Cook time: 14 minutes per batch | Serves 4

Cooking oil spray	1 teaspoon freshly ground black
4 (110 g) sirloin steaks	pepper, divided
1 teaspoon granulated garlic,	4 eggs
divided	½ teaspoon paprika
1 teaspoon salt, divided	

1. Insert the crisper plate into the basket and the basket into the unit. Preheat the unit by selecting AIR FRY, setting the temperature to 180°C, and setting the time to 3 minutes. Select START/STOP to begin. 2. Once the unit is preheated, spray the crisper plate with cooking oil. Place 2 steaks into the basket; do not oil or season them at this time. 3. Select AIR FRY, set the temperature to 180°C, and set the time to 9 minutes. Select START/STOP to begin. 4. After 5 minutes, open the unit and flip the steaks. Sprinkle each with ¼ teaspoon of granulated garlic, ¼ teaspoon of salt, and ¼ teaspoon of pepper. Resume cooking until the steaks register at least 65°C on a food thermometer. 5. When the cooking is complete, transfer the steaks to a plate and tent with aluminum foil to keep warm. Repeat steps 2, 3, and 4 with the remaining steaks. 6. Spray 4 ramekins with olive oil. Crack 1 egg into each ramekin. Sprinkle the eggs with the paprika and remaining ½ teaspoon each of salt and pepper. Working in batches, place 2 ramekins into the basket. 7. Select BAKE, set the temperature to 165°C, and set the time to 5 minutes. Select START/STOP to begin. 8. When the cooking is complete and the eggs are cooked to 70°C, remove the ramekins and repeat step 7 with the remaining 2 ramekins. 9. Serve the eggs with the steaks.

Smoky Sausage Patties

Prep time: 30 minutes | Cook time: 9 minutes | Serves 8

450 g pork mince	½ teaspoon fennel seeds
1 tablespoon soy sauce or	½ teaspoon dried thyme
tamari	½ teaspoon freshly ground
1 teaspoon smoked paprika	black pepper
1 teaspoon dried sage	¼ teaspoon cayenne pepper
1 teaspoon sea salt	

1. In a large bowl, combine the pork, soy sauce, smoked paprika, sage, salt, fennel seeds, thyme, black pepper, and cayenne pepper. Work the meat with your hands until the seasonings are fully incorporated. 2. Shape the mixture into 8 equal-size patties. Using your thumb, make a dent in the center of each patty. Place the patties on a plate and cover with plastic wrap. Refrigerate the patties for at least 30 minutes. 3. Working in batches if necessary, place the patties in a single layer in the air fryer, being careful not to overcrowd them. 4. Set the air fryer to 200°C and air fry for 5 minutes. Flip and cook for about 4 minutes more.

Easy Sausage Pizza

Prep time: 10 minutes | Cook time: 6 minutes | Serves 4

2 tablespoons ketchup	230 g Mozzarella cheese
1 pitta bread	1 teaspoon garlic powder
80 ml sausage meat	1 tablespoon olive oil

1. Preheat the air fryer to 170°C. 2. Spread the ketchup over the pitta bread. 3. Top with the sausage meat and cheese. Sprinkle with the garlic powder and olive oil. 4. Put the pizza in the air fryer basket and bake for 6 minutes. 5. Serve warm.

Bacon, Cheese, and Avocado Melt

Prep time: 5 minutes | Cook time: 3 to 5 minutes | Serves 2

1 avocado	1 tablespoon double cream
4 slices cooked bacon, chopped	60 ml shredded Cheddar cheese
2 tablespoons salsa	

1. Preheat the air fryer to 200°C. 2. Slice the avocado in half lengthwise and remove the stone. To ensure the avocado halves do not roll in the basket, slice a thin piece of skin off the base. 3. In a small bowl, combine the bacon, salsa, and cream. Divide the mixture between the avocado halves and top with the cheese. 4. Place the avocado halves in the air fryer basket and air fry for 3 to 5 minutes until the cheese has melted and begins to brown. Serve warm.

Three-Berry Dutch Pancake

Prep time: 10 minutes | Cook time: 12 to 16 minutes | Serves 4

2 egg whites
1 egg
120 ml wholemeal plain flour plus 1 tablespoon cornflour
120 ml semi-skimmed milk
1 teaspoon pure vanilla extract
1 tablespoon unsalted butter, melted
235 ml sliced fresh strawberries
120 ml fresh blueberries
120 ml fresh raspberries

1. In a medium bowl, use an eggbeater or hand mixer to quickly mix the egg whites, egg, flour, milk, and vanilla until well combined. 2. Use a pastry brush to grease the bottom of a baking pan with the melted butter. Immediately pour in the batter and put the basket back in the fryer. Bake at 165ºC for 12 to 16 minutes, or until the pancake is puffed and golden brown. 3. Remove the pan from the air fryer; the pancake will fall. Top with the strawberries, blueberries, and raspberries. Serve immediately.

Buffalo Chicken Breakfast Muffins

Prep time: 7 minutes | Cook time: 13 to 16 minutes | Serves 10

170 g shredded cooked chicken
85 g blue cheese, crumbled
2 tablespoons unsalted butter, melted
80 ml Buffalo hot sauce, such as Frank's RedHot
1 teaspoon minced garlic
6 large eggs
Sea salt and freshly ground black pepper, to taste
Avocado oil spray

1. In a large bowl, stir together the chicken, blue cheese, melted butter, hot sauce, and garlic. 2. In a medium bowl or large liquid measuring cup, beat the eggs. Season with salt and pepper. 3. Spray 10 silicone muffin cups with oil. Divide the chicken mixture among the cups, and pour the egg mixture over top. 4. Place the cups in the air fryer and set to 150ºC. Bake for 13 to 16 minutes, until the muffins are set and cooked through. (Depending on the size of your air fryer, you may need to cook the muffins in batches.)

Pitta and Pepperoni Pizza

Prep time: 10 minutes | Cook time: 6 minutes | Serves 1

1 teaspoon olive oil
1 tablespoon pizza sauce
1 pitta bread
6 pepperoni slices
60 ml grated Mozzarella cheese
¼ teaspoon garlic powder
¼ teaspoon dried oregano

1. Preheat the air fryer to 175ºC. Grease the air fryer basket with olive oil. 2. Spread the pizza sauce on top of the pitta bread. Put the pepperoni slices over the sauce, followed by the Mozzarella cheese. 3. Season with garlic powder and oregano. 4. Put the pitta pizza inside the air fryer and place a trivet on top. 5. Bake in the preheated air fryer for 6 minutes and serve.

Spinach and Swiss Frittata with Mushrooms

Prep time: 10 minutes | Cook time: 20 minutes | Serves 4

Olive oil cooking spray
8 large eggs
½ teaspoon salt
½ teaspoon black pepper
1 garlic clove, minced
475 ml fresh baby spinach
110 g baby mushrooms, sliced
1 shallot, diced
120 ml shredded Swiss cheese, divided
Hot sauce, for serving (optional)

1. Preheat the air fryer to 180ºC. Lightly coat the inside of a 6-inch round cake pan with olive oil cooking spray. 2. In a large bowl, beat the eggs, salt, pepper, and garlic for 1 to 2 minutes, or until well combined. 3. Fold in the spinach, mushrooms, shallot, and 60 ml the Swiss cheese. 4. Pour the egg mixture into the prepared cake pan, and sprinkle the remaining 60 ml Swiss over the top. 5. Place into the air fryer and bake for 18 to 20 minutes, or until the eggs are set in the center. 6. Remove from the air fryer and allow to cool for 5 minutes. Drizzle with hot sauce (if using) before serving.

Pork Sausage Eggs with Mustard Sauce

Prep time: 20 minutes | Cook time: 12 minutes | Serves 8

450 g pork sausage meat
8 soft-boiled or hard-boiled eggs, peeled
1 large egg
2 tablespoons milk
235 ml crushed pork scratchings
Smoky Mustard Sauce:
60 ml mayonnaise
2 tablespoons sour cream
1 tablespoon Dijon mustard
1 teaspoon chipotle hot sauce

1. Preheat the air fryer to 200ºC. 2. Divide the sausage into 8 portions. Take each portion of sausage, pat it down into a patty, and place 1 egg in the middle, gently wrapping the sausage around the egg until the egg is completely covered. (Wet your hands slightly if you find the sausage to be too sticky.) Repeat with the remaining eggs and sausage. 3. In a small shallow bowl, whisk the egg and milk until frothy. In another shallow bowl, place the crushed pork scratchings. Working one at a time, dip a sausage-wrapped egg into the beaten egg and then into the pork scratchings, gently rolling to coat evenly. Repeat with the remaining sausage-wrapped eggs. 4. Arrange the eggs in a single layer in the air fryer basket, and lightly spray with olive oil. Air fry for 10 to 12 minutes, pausing halfway through the baking time to turn the eggs, until the eggs are hot and the sausage is cooked through. 5. To make the sauce: In a small bowl, combine the mayonnaise, sour cream, Dijon, and hot sauce. Whisk until thoroughly combined. Serve with the Scotch eggs.

Cajun Breakfast Sausage

Prep time: 10 minutes | Cook time: 15 to 20 minutes | Serves 8

680 g 85% lean turkey mince	1 teaspoon Cajun seasoning
3 cloves garlic, finely chopped	1 teaspoon dried thyme
¼ onion, grated	½ teaspoon paprika
1 teaspoon Tabasco sauce	½ teaspoon cayenne

1. Preheat the air fryer to 190ºC. 2. In a large bowl, combine the turkey, garlic, onion, Tabasco, Cajun seasoning, thyme, paprika, and cayenne. Mix with clean hands until thoroughly combined. Shape into 16 patties, about ½ inch thick. (Wet your hands slightly if you find the sausage too sticky to handle.) 3. Working in batches if necessary, arrange the patties in a single layer in the air fryer basket. Pausing halfway through the cooking time to flip the patties, air fry for 15 to 20 minutes until a thermometer inserted into the thickest portion registers 75ºC.

Lemon-Blueberry Muffins

Prep time: 5 minutes | Cook time: 20 to 25 minutes | Makes 6

muffins	2 large eggs
300 ml almond flour	3 tablespoons melted butter
3 tablespoons granulated sweetener	1 tablespoon almond milk
	1 tablespoon fresh lemon juice
1 teaspoon baking powder	120 ml fresh blueberries

1. Preheat the air fryer to 175ºC. Lightly coat 6 silicone muffin cups with vegetable oil. Set aside. 2. In a large mixing bowl, combine the almond flour, sweetener, and baking soda. Set aside. 3. In a separate small bowl, whisk together the eggs, butter, milk, and lemon juice. Add the egg mixture to the flour mixture and stir until just combined. Fold in the blueberries and let the batter sit for 5 minutes. 4. Spoon the muffin batter into the muffin cups, about two-thirds full. Air fry for 20 to 25 minutes, or until a toothpick inserted into the center of a muffin comes out clean. 5. Remove the basket from the air fryer and let the muffins cool for about 5 minutes before transferring them to a wire rack to cool completely.

Mushroom-and-Tomato Stuffed Hash Browns

Prep time: 10 minutes | Cook time: 20 minutes | Serves 4

Olive oil cooking spray	1 garlic clove, minced
1 tablespoon plus 2 teaspoons olive oil, divided	475 ml shredded potatoes
	½ teaspoon salt
110 g baby mushrooms, diced	¼ teaspoon black pepper
1 spring onion, white parts and green parts, diced	1 plum tomato, diced
	120 ml shredded mozzarella

1. Preheat the air fryer to 190ºC. Lightly coat the inside of a 6-inch

cake pan with olive oil cooking spray. 2. In a small skillet, heat 2 teaspoons olive oil over medium heat. Add the mushrooms, spring onion, and garlic, and cook for 4 to 5 minutes, or until they have softened and are beginning to show some color. Remove from heat. 3. Meanwhile, in a large bowl, combine the potatoes, salt, pepper, and the remaining tablespoon olive oil. Toss until all potatoes are well coated. 4. Pour half of the potatoes into the bottom of the cake pan. Top with the mushroom mixture, tomato, and mozzarella. Spread the remaining potatoes over the top. 5. Bake in the air fryer for 12 to 15 minutes, or until the top is golden brown. 6. Remove from the air fryer and allow to cool for 5 minutes before slicing and serving.

Kale and Potato Nuggets

Prep time: 10 minutes | Cook time: 18 minutes | Serves 4

1 teaspoon extra virgin olive oil	30 ml milk
1 clove garlic, minced	Salt and ground black pepper, to taste
1 L kale, rinsed and chopped	
475 ml potatoes, boiled and mashed	Cooking spray

1. Preheat the air fryer to 200ºC. 2. In a skillet over medium heat, sauté the garlic in the olive oil, until it turns golden brown. Sauté with the kale for an additional 3 minutes and remove from the heat. 3. Mix the mashed potatoes, kale and garlic in a bowl. Pour in the milk and sprinkle with salt and pepper. 4. Shape the mixture into nuggets and spritz with cooking spray. 5. Put in the air fryer basket and air fry for 15 minutes, flip the nuggets halfway through cooking to make sure the nuggets fry evenly. 6. Serve immediately.

Chimichanga Breakfast Burrito

Prep time: 10 minutes | Cook time: 10 minutes | Serves 2

2 large (10- to 12-inch) flour tortillas	4 corn tortilla chips, crushed
	120 ml grated chili cheese
120 ml canned refried beans (pinto or black work equally well)	12 pickled jalapeño slices
	1 tablespoon vegetable oil
4 large eggs, cooked scrambled	Guacamole, salsa, and sour cream, for serving (optional)

1. Place the tortillas on a work surface and divide the refried beans between them, spreading them in a rough rectangle in the center of the tortillas. Top the beans with the scrambled eggs, crushed chips, cheese, and jalapeños. Fold one side over the fillings, then fold in each short side and roll up the rest of the way like a burrito. 2. Brush the outside of the burritos with the oil, then transfer to the air fryer, seam-side down. Air fry at 175ºC until the tortillas are browned and crisp and the filling is warm throughout, about 10 minutes. 3. Transfer the chimichangas to plates and serve warm with guacamole, salsa, and sour cream, if you like.

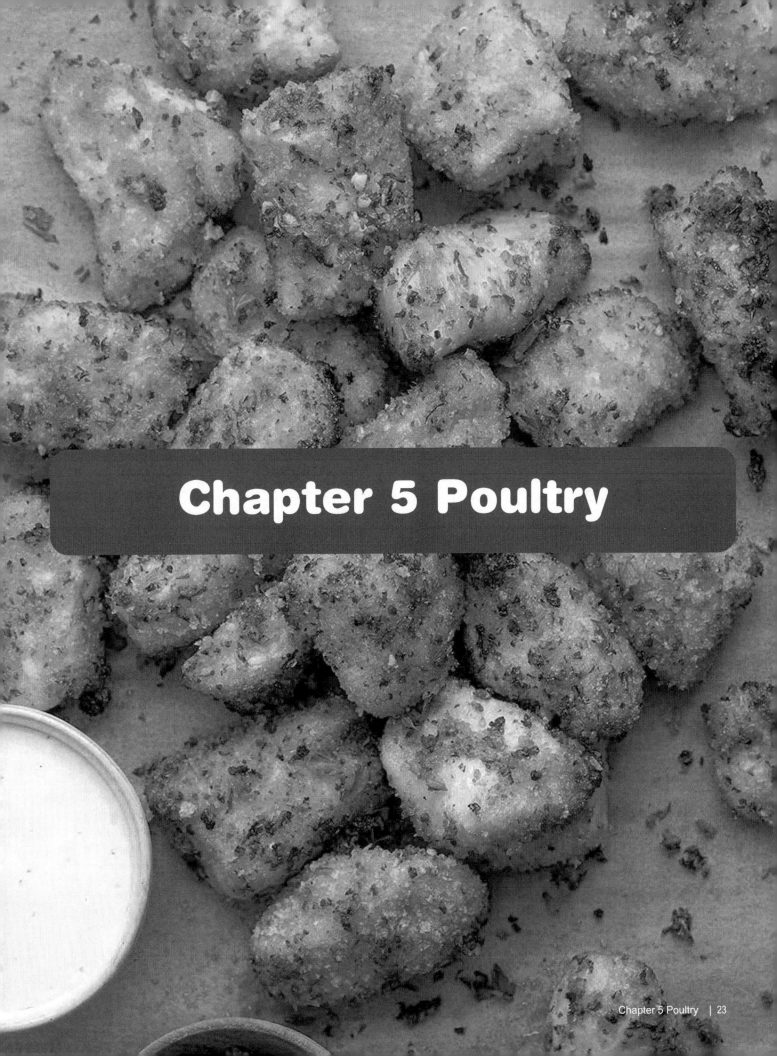

Chapter 5 Poultry

Chapter 5 Poultry

Chicken Shawarma

Prep time: 30 minutes | Cook time: 15 minutes | Serves 4

Shawarma Spice:
2 teaspoons dried oregano
1 teaspoon ground cinnamon
1 teaspoon ground cumin
1 teaspoon ground coriander
1 teaspoon kosher salt
½ teaspoon ground allspice
½ teaspoon cayenne pepper

Chicken:
450 g boneless, skinless chicken thighs, cut into large bite-size chunks
2 tablespoons vegetable oil
For Serving:
Tzatziki
Pita bread

1. For the shawarma spice: In a small bowl, combine the oregano, cayenne, cumin, coriander, salt, cinnamon, and allspice. 2. For the chicken: In a large bowl, toss together the chicken, vegetable oil, and shawarma spice to coat. Marinate at room temperature for 30 minutes or cover and refrigerate for up to 24 hours. 3. Place the chicken in the air fryer basket. Set the air fryer to 180ºC for 15 minutes, or until the chicken reaches an internal temperature of 75ºC. 4. Transfer the chicken to a serving platter. Serve with tzatziki and pita bread.

Turkey Meatloaf

Prep time: 10 minutes | Cook time: 50 minutes | Serves 4

230 g sliced mushrooms
1 small onion, coarsely chopped
2 cloves garlic
680 g 85% lean turkey mince
2 eggs, lightly beaten
1 tablespoon tomato paste
25 g almond meal

2 tablespoons almond milk
1 tablespoon dried oregano
1 teaspoon salt
½ teaspoon freshly ground black pepper
1 Roma tomato, thinly sliced

1. Preheat the air fryer to 180ºC. . Lightly coat a round pan with olive oil and set aside. 2. In a food processor fitted with a metal blade, combine the mushrooms, onion, and garlic. Pulse until finely chopped. Transfer the vegetables to a large mixing bowl. 3. Add the turkey, eggs, tomato paste, almond meal, milk, oregano, salt, and black pepper. Mix gently until thoroughly combined. Transfer the mixture to the prepared pan and shape into a loaf. Arrange the tomato slices on top. 4. Air fry for 50 minutes or until the meatloaf is nicely browned and a thermometer inserted into the thickest part registers 75ºC. Remove from the air fryer and let rest for about 10 minutes before slicing.

Chicken, Courgette, and Spinach Salad

Prep time: 10 minutes | Cook time: 20 minutes | Serves 4

3 (140 g) boneless, skinless chicken breasts, cut into 1-inch cubes
5 teaspoons extra-virgin olive oil
½ teaspoon dried thyme

1 medium red onion, sliced
1 red bell pepper, sliced
1 small courgette, cut into strips
3 tablespoons freshly squeezed lemon juice
85 g fresh baby spinach leaves

1. Insert the crisper plate into the basket and the basket into the unit. Preheat the unit by selecting AIR ROAST, setting the temperature to 190ºC, and setting the time to 3 minutes. Select START/STOP to begin. 2. In a large bowl, combine the chicken, olive oil, and thyme. Toss to coat. Transfer to a medium metal bowl that fits into the basket. 3. Once the unit is preheated, place the bowl into the basket. 4. Select AIR ROAST, set the temperature to 190ºC, and set the time to 20 minutes. Select START/STOP to begin. 5. After 8 minutes, add the red onion, red bell pepper, and courgette to the bowl. Resume cooking. After about 6 minutes more, stir the chicken and vegetables. Resume cooking. 6. When the cooking is complete, a food thermometer inserted into the chicken should register at least 75ºC. Remove the bowl from the unit and stir in the lemon juice. 7. Put the spinach in a serving bowl and top with the chicken mixture. Toss to combine and serve immediately.

Buffalo Chicken Cheese Sticks

Prep time: 5 minutes | Cook time: 8 minutes | Serves 2

140 g shredded cooked chicken
60 ml buffalo sauce
220 g shredded Mozzarella

cheese
1 large egg
55 g crumbled feta

1. In a large bowl, mix all ingredients except the feta. Cut a piece of parchment to fit your air fryer basket and press the mixture into a ½-inch-thick circle. 2. Sprinkle the mixture with feta and place into the air fryer basket. 3. Adjust the temperature to 200ºC and air fry for 8 minutes. 4. After 5 minutes, flip over the cheese mixture. 5. Allow to cool 5 minutes before cutting into sticks. Serve warm.

Cranberry Curry Chicken

Prep time: 12 minutes | Cook time: 18 minutes | Serves 4

3 (140 g) low-sodium boneless, skinless chicken breasts, cut into 1½-inch cubes
2 teaspoons olive oil
2 tablespoons cornflour
1 tablespoon curry powder
1 tart apple, chopped

120 ml low-sodium chicken broth
60 g dried cranberries
2 tablespoons freshly squeezed orange juice
Brown rice, cooked (optional)

1. Preheat the air fryer to 195ºC. 2. In a medium bowl, mix the chicken and olive oil. Sprinkle with the cornflour and curry powder. Toss to coat. Stir in the apple and transfer to a metal pan. Bake in the air fryer for 8 minutes, stirring once during cooking. 3. Add the chicken broth, cranberries, and orange juice. Bake for about 10 minutes more, or until the sauce is slightly thickened and the chicken reaches an internal temperature of 75ºC on a meat thermometer. Serve over hot cooked brown rice, if desired.

Spinach and Feta Stuffed Chicken Breasts

Prep time: 10 minutes | Cook time: 27 minutes | Serves 4

1 (280 g) package frozen spinach, thawed and drained well
80 g feta cheese, crumbled
½ teaspoon freshly ground

black pepper
4 boneless chicken breasts
Salt and freshly ground black pepper, to taste
1 tablespoon olive oil

1. Prepare the filling. Squeeze out as much liquid as possible from the thawed spinach. Rough chop the spinach and transfer it to a mixing bowl with the feta cheese and the freshly ground black pepper. 2. Prepare the chicken breast. Place the chicken breast on a cutting board and press down on the chicken breast with one hand to keep it stabilized. Make an incision about 1-inch long in the fattest side of the breast. Move the knife up and down inside the chicken breast, without poking through either the top or the bottom, or the other side of the breast. The inside pocket should be about 3-inches long, but the opening should only be about 1-inch wide. If this is too difficult, you can make the incision longer, but you will have to be more careful when cooking the chicken breast since this will expose more of the stuffing. 3. Once you have prepared the chicken breasts, use your fingers to stuff the filling into each pocket, spreading the mixture down as far as you can. 4. Preheat the air fryer to 190ºC. 5. Lightly brush or spray the air fryer basket and the chicken breasts with olive oil. Transfer two of the stuffed chicken breasts to the air fryer. Air fry for 12 minutes, turning the chicken breasts over halfway through the cooking time. Remove the chicken to a resting plate and air fry the second two breasts for 12 minutes. Return the first batch of chicken to the air fryer with the second batch and air fry for 3 more minutes. When the chicken is cooked, an instant read thermometer should register 75ºC in the thickest part of the chicken, as well as in the stuffing. 6. Remove the chicken breasts and let them rest on a cutting board for 2 to 3 minutes. Slice the chicken on the bias and serve with the slices fanned out.

Brazilian Tempero Baiano Chicken Drumsticks

Prep time: 30 minutes | Cook time: 20 minutes | Serves 4

1 teaspoon cumin seeds
1 teaspoon dried oregano
1 teaspoon dried parsley
1 teaspoon ground turmeric
½ teaspoon coriander seeds
1 teaspoon kosher salt

½ teaspoon black peppercorns
½ teaspoon cayenne pepper
60 ml fresh lime juice
2 tablespoons olive oil
680 g chicken drumsticks

1. In a clean coffee grinder or spice mill, combine the cumin, oregano, parsley, turmeric, coriander seeds, salt, peppercorns, and cayenne. Process until finely ground. 2. In a small bowl, combine the ground spices with the lime juice and oil. Place the chicken in a resealable plastic bag. Add the marinade, seal, and massage until the chicken is well coated. Marinate at room temperature for 30 minutes or in the refrigerator for up to 24 hours. 3. When you are ready to cook, place the drumsticks skin side up in the air fryer basket. Set the air fryer to 200ºC for 20 to 25 minutes, turning the legs halfway through the cooking time. Use a meat thermometer to ensure that the chicken has reached an internal temperature of 75ºC. 4. Serve with plenty of napkins.

Spice-Rubbed Turkey Breast

Prep time: 5 minutes | Cook time: 45 to 55 minutes | Serves 10

1 tablespoon sea salt
1 teaspoon paprika
1 teaspoon onion powder
1 teaspoon garlic powder
½ teaspoon freshly ground

black pepper
1.8 kg bone-in, skin-on turkey breast
2 tablespoons unsalted butter, melted

1. In a small bowl, combine the salt, paprika, onion powder, garlic powder, and pepper. 2. Sprinkle the seasonings all over the turkey. Brush the turkey with some of the melted butter. 3. Set the air fryer to 180ºC. . Place the turkey in the air fryer basket, skin-side down, and roast for 25 minutes. 4. Flip the turkey and brush it with the remaining butter. Continue cooking for another 20 to 30 minutes, until an instant-read thermometer reads 70ºC. 5. Remove the turkey breast from the air fryer. Tent a piece of aluminum foil over the turkey, and allow it to rest for about 5 minutes before serving.

Hoisin Turkey Burgers

Prep time: 30 minutes | Cook time: 20 minutes | Serves 4

Olive oil	60 ml hoisin sauce
450 g lean turkey mince	2 tablespoons soy sauce
30 g whole-wheat bread crumbs	4 whole-wheat buns

1. Spray the air fryer basket lightly with olive oil. 2. In a large bowl, mix together the turkey, bread crumbs, hoisin sauce, and soy sauce. 3. Form the mixture into 4 equal patties. Cover with plastic wrap and refrigerate the patties for 30 minutes. 4. Place the patties in the air fryer basket in a single layer. Spray the patties lightly with olive oil. 5. Air fry at 190°C for 10 minutes. Flip the patties over, lightly spray with olive oil, and cook until golden brown, an additional 5 to 10 minutes. 6. Place the patties on buns and top with your choice of low-calorie burger toppings like sliced tomatoes, onions, and cabbage slaw.

Pomegranate-Glazed Chicken with Couscous Salad

Prep time: 25 minutes | Cook time: 20 minutes | Serves 4

3 tablespoons plus 2 teaspoons pomegranate molasses	80 g couscous
½ teaspoon ground cinnamon	1 tablespoon minced fresh parsley
1 teaspoon minced fresh thyme	60 g cherry tomatoes, quartered
Salt and ground black pepper, to taste	1 scallion, white part minced, green part sliced thin on bias
2 (340 g) bone-in split chicken breasts, trimmed	1 tablespoon extra-virgin olive oil
60 ml chicken broth	30 g feta cheese, crumbled
60 ml water	Cooking spray

1. Preheat the air fryer to 180°C. Spritz the air fryer basket with cooking spray. 2. Combine 3 tablespoons of pomegranate molasses, cinnamon, thyme, and ⅛ teaspoon of salt in a small bowl. Stir to mix well. Set aside. 3. Place the chicken breasts in the preheated air fryer, skin side down, and spritz with cooking spray. Sprinkle with salt and ground black pepper. 4. Air fry the chicken for 10 minutes, then brush the chicken with half of pomegranate molasses mixture and flip. Air fry for 5 more minutes. 5. Brush the chicken with remaining pomegranate molasses mixture and flip. Air fry for another 5 minutes or until the internal temperature of the chicken breasts reaches at least 75°C. 6. Meanwhile, pour the broth and water in a pot and bring to a boil over medium-high heat. Add the couscous and sprinkle with salt. Cover and simmer for 7 minutes or until the liquid is almost absorbed. 7. Combine the remaining ingredients, except for the cheese, with cooked couscous in a large bowl. Toss to mix well. Scatter with the feta cheese. 8. When the air frying is complete, remove the chicken from the air fryer and allow to cool for 10 minutes. Serve with vegetable and couscous salad.

Porchetta-Style Chicken Breasts

Prep time: 10 minutes | Cook time: 15 minutes | Serves 4

25 g fresh parsley leaves	1 teaspoon ground fennel
10 g roughly chopped fresh chives	½ teaspoon red pepper flakes
4 cloves garlic, peeled	4 (115 g) boneless, skinless chicken breasts, pounded to ¼ inch thick
2 tablespoons lemon juice	8 slices bacon
3 teaspoons fine sea salt	Sprigs of fresh rosemary, for garnish (optional)
1 teaspoon dried rubbed sage	
1 teaspoon fresh rosemary leaves	

1. Spray the air fryer basket with avocado oil. Preheat the air fryer to 170°C. 2. Place the parsley, chives, garlic, lemon juice, salt, sage, rosemary, fennel, and red pepper flakes in a food processor and purée until a smooth paste forms. 3. Place the chicken breasts on a cutting board and rub the paste all over the tops. With a short end facing you, roll each breast up like a jelly roll to make a log and secure it with toothpicks. 4. Wrap 2 slices of bacon around each chicken breast log to cover the entire breast. Secure the bacon with toothpicks. 5. Place the chicken breast logs in the air fryer basket and air fry for 5 minutes, flip the logs over, and cook for another 5 minutes. Increase the heat to 200°C and cook until the bacon is crisp, about 5 minutes more. 6. Remove the toothpicks and garnish with fresh rosemary sprigs, if desired, before serving. Store leftovers in an airtight container in the refrigerator for up to 4 days or in the freezer for up to a month. Reheat in a preheated 180°C air fryer for 5 minutes, then increase the heat to 200°C and cook for 2 minutes to crisp the bacon.

Tex-Mex Chicken Breasts

Prep time: 10 minutes | Cook time: 17 to 20 minutes | Serves 4

450 g low-sodium boneless, skinless chicken breasts, cut into 1-inch cubes	2 teaspoons olive oil
1 medium onion, chopped	115 g canned low-sodium black beans, rinsed and drained
1 red bell pepper, chopped	130 g low-sodium salsa
1 jalapeño pepper, minced	2 teaspoons chili powder

1. Preheat the air fryer to 200°C. 2. In a medium metal bowl, mix the chicken, onion, bell pepper, jalapeño, and olive oil. Roast for 10 minutes, stirring once during cooking. 3. Add the black beans, salsa, and chili powder. Roast for 7 to 10 minutes more, stirring once, until the chicken reaches an internal temperature of 75°C on a meat thermometer. Serve immediately.

Chicken and Vegetable Fajitas

Prep time: 15 minutes | Cook time: 23 minutes | Serves 6

Chicken:
450 g boneless, skinless chicken thighs, cut crosswise into thirds
1 tablespoon vegetable oil
4½ teaspoons taco seasoning
Vegetables:
50 g sliced onion
150 g sliced bell pepper
1 or 2 jalapeños, quartered lengthwise

1 tablespoon vegetable oil
½ teaspoon kosher salt
½ teaspoon ground cumin
For Serving:
Tortillas
Sour cream
Shredded cheese
Guacamole
Salsa

1. For the chicken: In a medium bowl, toss together the chicken, vegetable oil, and taco seasoning to coat. 2. For the vegetables: In a separate bowl, toss together the onion, bell pepper, jalapeño(s), vegetable oil, salt, and cumin to coat. 3. Place the chicken in the air fryer basket. Set the air fryer to (190ºC for 10 minutes. Add the vegetables to the basket, toss everything together to blend the seasonings, and set the air fryer for 13 minutes more. Use a meat thermometer to ensure the chicken has reached an internal temperature of 75ºC. 4. Transfer the chicken and vegetables to a serving platter. Serve with tortillas and the desired fajita fixings.

Bacon Lovers' Stuffed Chicken

Prep time: 15 minutes | Cook time: 10 minutes | Serves 4

4 (140 g) boneless, skinless chicken breasts, pounded to ¼ inch thick
2 (150 g) packages Boursin cheese (or Kite Hill brand chive cream cheese style spread,

softened, for dairy-free)
8 slices thin-cut bacon or beef bacon
Sprig of fresh coriander, for garnish (optional)

1. Spray the air fryer basket with avocado oil. Preheat the air fryer to 200ºC. 2. Place one of the chicken breasts on a cutting board. With a sharp knife held parallel to the cutting board, make a 1-inch-wide incision at the top of the breast. Carefully cut into the breast to form a large pocket, leaving a ½-inch border along the sides and bottom. Repeat with the other 3 chicken breasts. 3. Snip the corner of a large resealable plastic bag to form a ¾-inch hole. Place the Boursin cheese in the bag and pipe the cheese into the pockets in the chicken breasts, dividing the cheese evenly among them. 4. Wrap 2 slices of bacon around each chicken breast and secure the ends with toothpicks. Place the bacon-wrapped chicken in the air fryer basket and air fry until the bacon is crisp and the chicken's internal temperature reaches 75ºC, about 18 to 20 minutes, flipping after 10 minutes. Garnish with a sprig of coriander before serving, if desired. 5. Store leftovers in an airtight container in the refrigerator for up to 4 days. Reheat in a preheated 200ºC air fryer for 5 minutes, or until warmed through.

Sriracha-Honey Chicken Nuggets

Prep time: 15 minutes | Cook time: 19 minutes | Serves 6

Oil, for spraying
1 large egg
180 ml milk
125 g all-purpose flour
2 tablespoons icing sugar
½ teaspoon paprika
½ teaspoon salt

½ teaspoon freshly ground black pepper
2 boneless, skinless chicken breasts, cut into bite-size pieces
140 g barbecue sauce
2 tablespoons honey
1 tablespoon Sriracha

1. Line the air fryer basket with parchment and spray lightly with oil. 2. In a small bowl, whisk together the egg and milk. 3. In a medium bowl, combine the flour, icing sugar, paprika, salt, and black pepper and stir. 4. Coat the chicken in the egg mixture, then dredge in the flour mixture until evenly coated. 5. Place the chicken in the prepared basket and spray liberally with oil. 6. Air fry at 200ºC for 8 minutes, flip, spray with more oil, and cook for another 6 to 8 minutes, or until the internal temperature reaches 75ºC and the juices run clear. 7. In a large bowl, mix together the barbecue sauce, honey, and Sriracha. 8. Transfer the chicken to the bowl and toss until well coated with the barbecue sauce mixture. 9. Line the air fryer basket with fresh parchment, return the chicken to the basket, and cook for another 2 to 3 minutes, until browned and crispy.

Curried Orange Honey Chicken

Prep time: 10 minutes | Cook time: 16 to 19 minutes | Serves 4

340 g boneless, skinless chicken thighs, cut into 1-inch pieces
1 yellow bell pepper, cut into 1½-inch pieces
1 small red onion, sliced
Olive oil for misting

60 ml chicken stock
2 tablespoons honey
60 ml orange juice
1 tablespoon cornflour
2 to 3 teaspoons curry powder

1. Preheat the air fryer to 190ºC. 2. Put the chicken thighs, pepper, and red onion in the air fryer basket and mist with olive oil. 3. Roast for 12 to 14 minutes or until the chicken is cooked to 75ºC, shaking the basket halfway through cooking time. 4. Remove the chicken and vegetables from the air fryer basket and set aside. 5. In a metal bowl, combine the stock, honey, orange juice, cornflour, and curry powder, and mix well. Add the chicken and vegetables, stir, and put the bowl in the basket. 6. Return the basket to the air fryer and roast for 2 minutes. Remove and stir, then roast for 2 to 3 minutes or until the sauce is thickened and bubbly. 7. Serve warm.

Chicken Burgers with Ham and Cheese

Prep time: 12 minutes | Cook time: 13 to 16 minutes | Serves 4

40 g soft bread crumbs	taste
3 tablespoons milk	570 g chicken mince
1 egg, beaten	70 g finely chopped ham
½ teaspoon dried thyme	75 g grated Gouda cheese
Pinch salt	Olive oil for misting
Freshly ground black pepper, to	

1. Preheat the air fryer to 180ºC. 2. In a medium bowl, combine the bread crumbs, milk, egg, thyme, salt, and pepper. Add the chicken and mix gently but thoroughly with clean hands. 3. Form the chicken into eight thin patties and place on waxed paper. 4. Top four of the patties with the ham and cheese. Top with remaining four patties and gently press the edges together to seal, so the ham and cheese mixture is in the middle of the burger. 5. Place the burgers in the basket and mist with olive oil. Bake for 13 to 16 minutes or until the chicken is thoroughly cooked to 75ºC as measured with a meat thermometer. Serve immediately.

Ethiopian Chicken with Cauliflower

Prep time: 15 minutes | Cook time: 28 minutes | Serves 6

2 handful fresh Italian parsley, roughly chopped	⅓ teaspoon porcini powder
20 g fresh chopped chives	1½ teaspoons berbere spice
2 sprigs thyme	⅓ teaspoon sweet paprika
6 chicken drumsticks	½ teaspoon shallot powder
1½ small-sized head cauliflower, broken into large-sized florets	1teaspoon granulated garlic
	1 teaspoon freshly cracked pink peppercorns
2 teaspoons mustard powder	½ teaspoon sea salt

1. Simply combine all items for the berbere spice rub mix. After that, coat the chicken drumsticks with this rub mix on all sides. Transfer them to the baking dish. 2. Now, lower the cauliflower onto the chicken drumsticks. Add thyme, chives and Italian parsley and spritz everything with a pan spray. Transfer the baking dish to the preheated air fryer. 3. Next step, set the timer for 28 minutes; roast at 180ºC, turning occasionally. Bon appétit!

Ginger Turmeric Chicken Thighs

Prep time: 5 minutes | Cook time: 25 minutes | Serves 4

4 (115 g) boneless, skin-on chicken thighs	½ teaspoon salt
	½ teaspoon garlic powder
2 tablespoons coconut oil, melted	½ teaspoon ground ginger
	¼ teaspoon ground black pepper
½ teaspoon ground turmeric	

1. Place chicken thighs in a large bowl and drizzle with coconut oil. Sprinkle with remaining ingredients and toss to coat both sides of thighs. 2. Place thighs skin side up into ungreased air fryer basket. Adjust the temperature to 200ºC and air fry for 25 minutes. After 10 minutes, turn thighs. When 5 minutes remain, flip thighs once more. Chicken will be done when skin is golden brown and the internal temperature is at least 75ºC. Serve warm.

Garlic Soy Chicken Thighs

Prep time: 10 minutes | Cook time: 30 minutes | Serves 1 to 2

2 tablespoons chicken stock	2 large spring onions, cut into 2- to 3-inch batons, plus more, thinly sliced, for garnish
2 tablespoons reduced-sodium soy sauce	
1½ tablespoons sugar	2 bone-in, skin-on chicken thighs (198 to 225 g each)
4 garlic cloves, smashed and peeled	

1. Preheat the air fryer to 190ºC. 2. In a metal cake pan, combine the chicken stock, soy sauce, and sugar and stir until the sugar dissolves. Add the garlic cloves, spring onions, and chicken thighs, turning the thighs to coat them in the marinade, then resting them skin-side up. Place the pan in the air fryer and bake, flipping the thighs every 5 minutes after the first 10 minutes, until the chicken is cooked through and the marinade is reduced to a sticky glaze over the chicken, about 30 minutes. 3. Remove the pan from the air fryer and serve the chicken thighs warm, with any remaining glaze spooned over top and sprinkled with more sliced spring onions.

Chapter 6 Fish and Seafood

Chapter 6 Fish and Seafood

Catfish Bites

Prep time: 15 minutes | Cook time: 20 minutes | Serves 4

Olive or vegetable oil, for spraying	70 g cornmeal
455 g catfish fillets, cut into 2-inch pieces	30 g plain flour
	2 teaspoons Creole seasoning
235 ml buttermilk	120 ml yellow mustard

1. Line the air fryer basket with baking paper and spray lightly with oil. 2. Place the catfish pieces and buttermilk in a zip-top plastic bag, seal, and refrigerate for about 10 minutes. 3. In a shallow bowl, mix together the cornmeal, flour, and Creole seasoning. 4. Remove the catfish from the bag and pat dry with a paper towel. 5. Spread the mustard on all sides of the catfish, then dip them in the cornmeal mixture until evenly coated. 6. Place the catfish in the prepared basket. You may need to work in batches, depending on the size of your air fryer. Spray lightly with oil. 7. Air fry at 200ºC for 10 minutes, flip carefully, spray with oil, and cook for another 10 minutes. Serve immediately.

Oyster Po'Boy

Prep time: 20 minutes | Cook time: 5 minutes | Serves 4

105 g plain flour	1 (12-inch) French baguette, quartered and sliced horizontally
40 g yellow cornmeal	
1 tablespoon Cajun seasoning	
1 teaspoon salt	Tartar Sauce, as needed
2 large eggs, beaten	150 g shredded lettuce, divided
1 teaspoon hot sauce	2 tomatoes, cut into slices
455 g pre-shucked oysters	Cooking spray

1. In a shallow bowl, whisk the flour, cornmeal, Cajun seasoning, and salt until blended. In a second shallow bowl, whisk together the eggs and hot sauce. 2. One at a time, dip the oysters in the cornmeal mixture, the eggs, and again in the cornmeal, coating thoroughly. 3. Preheat the air fryer to 200ºC. Line the air fryer basket with baking paper. 4. Place the oysters on the baking paper and spritz with oil. 5. Air fry for 2 minutes. Shake the basket, spritz the oysters with oil, and air fry for 3 minutes more until lightly browned and crispy. 6. Spread each sandwich half with Tartar Sauce. Assemble the po'boys by layering each sandwich with fried oysters, ½ cup shredded lettuce, and 2 tomato slices. 7. Serve immediately.

Scallops and Spinach with Cream Sauce

Prep time: 5 minutes | Cook time: 10 minutes | Serves 2

Vegetable oil spray	180 ml heavy cream
280 g frozen spinach, thawed and drained	1 tablespoon tomato paste
8 jumbo sea scallops	1 tablespoon chopped fresh basil
Kosher or coarse sea salt, and black pepper, to taste	1 teaspoon minced garlic

1. Spray a baking pan with vegetable oil spray. Spread the thawed spinach in an even layer in the bottom of the pan. 2. Spray both sides of the scallops with vegetable oil spray. Season lightly with salt and pepper. Arrange the scallops on top of the spinach. 3. In a small bowl, whisk together the cream, tomato paste, basil, garlic, ½ teaspoon salt, and ½ teaspoon pepper. Pour the sauce over the scallops and spinach. 4. Place the pan in the air fryer basket. Set the air fryer to 175ºC for 10 minutes. Use a meat thermometer to ensure the scallops have an internal temperature of 55ºC.

Crab and Bell Pepper Cakes

Prep time: 5 minutes | Cook time: 10 minutes | Serves 4

230 g jumbo lump crabmeat	1 egg
1 tablespoon Old Bay seasoning	60 g mayonnaise
40 g bread crumbs	Juice of ½ lemon
40 g diced red bell pepper	1 teaspoon plain flour
40 g diced green bell pepper	Cooking oil spray

1. Sort through the crabmeat, picking out any bits of shell or cartilage. 2. In a large bowl, stir together the Old Bay seasoning, bread crumbs, red and green bell peppers, egg, mayonnaise, and lemon juice. Gently stir in the crabmeat. 3. Insert the crisper plate into the basket and the basket into the unit. Preheat the unit to 190ºC. 4. Form the mixture into 4 patties. Sprinkle ¼ teaspoon of flour on top of each patty. 5. Once the unit is preheated, spray the crisper plate with cooking oil. Place the crab cakes into the basket and spray them with cooking oil. 6. Cook for 10 minutes. 7. When the cooking is complete, the crab cakes will be golden brown and firm.

Lemony Salmon

Prep time: 30 minutes | Cook time: 10 minutes | Serves 4

680 g salmon steak	garnish
½ teaspoon grated lemon zest	120 ml dry white wine, or apple
Freshly cracked mixed	cider vinegar
peppercorns, to taste	½ teaspoon fresh coriander,
80 ml lemon juice	chopped
Fresh chopped chives, for	Fine sea salt, to taste

1. To prepare the marinade, place all ingredients, except for salmon steak and chives, in a deep pan. Bring to a boil over medium-high flame until it has reduced by half. Allow it to cool down. 2. After that, allow salmon steak to marinate in the refrigerator approximately 40 minutes. Discard the marinade and transfer the fish steak to the preheated air fryer. 3. Air fry at 200ºC for 9 to 10 minutes. To finish, brush hot fish steaks with the reserved marinade, garnish with fresh chopped chives, and serve right away!

Firecracker Prawns

Prep time: 10 minutes | Cook time: 7 minutes | Serves 4

455 g medium prawns, peeled and deveined	2 tablespoons Sriracha
2 tablespoons salted butter, melted	¼ teaspoon powdered sweetener
½ teaspoon Old Bay seasoning	60 ml full-fat mayonnaise
¼ teaspoon garlic powder	⅛ teaspoon ground black pepper

1. In a large bowl, toss prawns in butter, Old Bay seasoning, and garlic powder. Place prawns into the air fryer basket. 2. Adjust the temperature to 200ºC and set the timer for 7 minutes. 3. Flip the prawns halfway through the cooking time. Prawns will be bright pink when fully cooked. 4. In another large bowl, mix Sriracha, sweetener, mayonnaise, and pepper. Toss prawns in the spicy mixture and serve immediately.

Crispy Herbed Salmon

Prep time: 5 minutes | Cook time: 9 to 12 minutes | Serves 4

4 skinless salmon fillets, 170 g each	½ teaspoon dried basil
3 tablespoons honey mustard	15 g panko bread crumbs
½ teaspoon dried thyme	30 g crushed ready salted crisps
	2 tablespoons olive oil

1. Place the salmon on a plate. In a small bowl, combine the mustard, thyme, and basil, and spread evenly over the salmon. 2. In another small bowl, combine the bread crumbs and crisps and mix well. Drizzle in the olive oil and mix until combined. 3. Place the salmon in the air fryer basket and gently but firmly press the bread crumb mixture onto the top of each fillet. 4. Bake at 160ºC for 9 to 12 minutes or until the salmon reaches at least 65ºC on a meat thermometer and the topping is browned and crisp.

Classic Fish Sticks with Tartar Sauce

Prep time: 10 minutes | Cook time: 12 to 15 minutes | Serves 4

680 g cod fillets, cut into 1-inch strips	120 ml sour cream
1 teaspoon salt	120 ml mayonnaise
½ teaspoon freshly ground black pepper	3 tablespoons chopped dill pickle
2 eggs	2 tablespoons capers, drained and chopped
70 g almond flour	½ teaspoon dried dill
20 g grated Parmesan cheese	1 tablespoon dill pickle liquid
Tartar Sauce:	(optional)

1. Preheat the air fryer to 200ºC. 2. Season the cod with the salt and black pepper; set aside. 3. In a shallow bowl, lightly beat the eggs. In a second shallow bowl, combine the almond flour and Parmesan cheese. Stir until thoroughly combined. 4. Working with a few pieces at a time, dip the fish into the egg mixture followed by the flour mixture. Press lightly to ensure an even coating. 5. Working in batches if necessary, arrange the fish in a single layer in the air fryer basket and spray lightly with olive oil. Pausing halfway through the cooking time to turn the fish, air fry for 12 to 15 minutes, until the fish flakes easily with a fork. Let sit in the basket for a few minutes before serving with the tartar sauce. 6. To make the tartar sauce: In a small bowl, combine the sour cream, mayonnaise, pickle, capers, and dill. If you prefer a thinner sauce, stir in the pickle liquid.

Italian Baked Cod

Prep time: 5 minutes | Cook time: 12 minutes | Serves 4

4 cod fillets, 170 g each	¼ teaspoon salt
2 tablespoons salted butter, melted	120 ml tomato-based pasta sauce
1 teaspoon Italian seasoning	

1. Place cod into an ungreased round nonstick baking dish. Pour butter over cod and sprinkle with Italian seasoning and salt. Top with pasta sauce. 2. Place dish into air fryer basket. Adjust the temperature to 175ºC and bake for 12 minutes. Fillets will be lightly browned, easily flake, and have an internal temperature of at least 65ºC when done. Serve warm.

Easy Scallops

Prep time: 5 minutes | Cook time: 4 minutes | Serves 2

12 medium sea scallops, rinsed and patted dry	pepper, plus more for garnish
1 teaspoon fine sea salt	Fresh thyme leaves, for garnish (optional)
¾ teaspoon ground black	Avocado oil spray

1. Preheat the air fryer to 200°C. Coat the air fryer basket with avocado oil spray. 2. Place the scallops in a medium bowl and spritz with avocado oil spray. Sprinkle the salt and pepper to season. 3. Transfer the seasoned scallops to the air fryer basket, spacing them apart. You may need to work in batches to avoid overcrowding. 4. Air fry for 4 minutes, flipping the scallops halfway through, or until the scallops are firm and reach an internal temperature of just 65°C on a meat thermometer. 5. Remove from the basket and repeat with the remaining scallops. 6. Sprinkle the pepper and thyme leaves on top for garnish, if desired. Serve immediately.

Stuffed Sole Florentine

Prep time: 10 minutes | Cook time: 25 minutes | Serves 4

40 g pine nuts	pepper, to taste
2 tablespoons olive oil	2 tablespoons unsalted butter, divided
90 g chopped tomatoes	
170 g bag spinach, coarsely chopped	4 Sole fillets (about 680 g)
2 cloves garlic, chopped	Dash of paprika
Salt and freshly ground black	½ lemon, sliced into 4 wedges

1. Place the pine nuts in a baking dish that fits in your air fryer. Set the air fryer to 200°C and air fry for 4 minutes until the nuts are lightly browned and fragrant. Remove the baking dish from the air fryer, tip the nuts onto a plate to cool, and continue preheating the air fryer. When the nuts are cool enough to handle, chop them into fine pieces. 2. In the baking dish, combine the oil, tomatoes, spinach, and garlic. Use tongs to toss until thoroughly combined. Air fry for 5 minutes until the tomatoes are softened and the spinach is wilted. 3. Transfer the vegetables to a bowl and stir in the toasted pine nuts. Season to taste with salt and freshly ground black pepper. 4. Place 1 tablespoon of the butter in the bottom of the baking dish. Lower the heat on the air fryer to 175°C. 5. Place the sole on a clean work surface. Sprinkle both sides with salt and black pepper. Divide the vegetable mixture among the sole fillets and carefully roll up, securing with toothpicks. 6. Working in batches if necessary, arrange the fillets seam-side down in the baking dish along with 1 tablespoon of water. Top the fillets with remaining 1 tablespoon butter and sprinkle with a dash of paprika. 7.Cover loosely with foil and air fry for 10 to 15 minutes until the fish is opaque and flakes easily with a fork. Remove the toothpicks before serving with the lemon wedges.

Prawn Caesar Salad

Prep time: 30 minutes | Cook time: 4 to 6 minutes | Serves 4

340 g fresh large prawns, peeled and deveined	¼ teaspoon freshly ground black pepper, plus additional to season the marinade
1 tablespoon plus 1 teaspoon freshly squeezed lemon juice, divided	
4 tablespoons olive oil or avocado oil, divided	735 g mayonnaise
	2 tablespoons freshly grated Parmesan cheese
2 garlic cloves, minced, divided	1 teaspoon Dijon mustard
¼ teaspoon sea salt, plus additional to season the marinade	1 tinned anchovy, mashed
	340 g romaine lettuce hearts, torn

1. Place the prawns in a large bowl. Add 1 tablespoon of lemon juice, 1 tablespoon of olive oil, and 1 minced garlic clove. Season with salt and pepper. Toss well and refrigerate for 15 minutes. 2. While the prawns marinates, make the dressing: In a blender, combine the mayonnaise, Parmesan cheese, Dijon mustard, the remaining 1 teaspoon of lemon juice, the anchovy, the remaining minced garlic clove, ¼ teaspoon of salt, and ¼ teaspoon of pepper. Process until smooth. With the blender running, slowly stream in the remaining 3 tablespoons of oil. Transfer the mixture to a jar; seal and refrigerate until ready to serve. 3. Remove the prawns from its marinade and place it in the air fryer basket in a single layer. Set the air fryer to 200°C and air fry for 2 minutes. Flip the prawns and cook for 2 to 4 minutes more, until the flesh turns opaque. 4. Place the romaine in a large bowl and toss with the desired amount of dressing. Top with the prawns and serve immediately.

Miso Salmon

Prep time: 10 minutes | Cook time: 12 minutes | Serves 2

2 tablespoons brown sugar	black pepper
2 tablespoons soy sauce	2 salmon fillets, 140 g each
2 tablespoons white miso paste	Vegetable oil spray
1 teaspoon minced garlic	1 teaspoon sesame seeds
1 teaspoon minced fresh ginger	2 spring onions, thinly sliced,
½ teaspoon freshly cracked	for garnish

1. In a small bowl, whisk together the brown sugar, soy sauce, miso, garlic, ginger, and pepper to combine. 2. Place the salmon fillets on a plate. Pour half the sauce over the fillets; turn the fillets to coat the other sides with sauce. 3. Spray the air fryer basket with vegetable oil spray. Place the sauce-covered salmon in the basket. Set the air fryer to 200°C for 12 minutes. Halfway through the cooking time, brush additional miso sauce on the salmon. 4. Sprinkle the salmon with the sesame seeds and spring onions and serve.

Sesame-Crusted Tuna Steak

Prep time: 5 minutes | Cook time: 8 minutes | Serves 2

2 tuna steaks, 170 g each	½ teaspoon garlic powder
1 tablespoon coconut oil, melted	2 teaspoons white sesame seeds
	2 teaspoons black sesame seeds

1. Brush each tuna steak with coconut oil and sprinkle with garlic powder. 2. In a large bowl, mix sesame seeds and then press each tuna steak into them, covering the steak as completely as possible. Place tuna steaks into the air fryer basket. 3. Adjust the temperature to 200ºC and air fry for 8 minutes. 4. Flip the steaks halfway through the cooking time. Steaks will be well-done at 65ºC internal temperature. Serve warm.

Cayenne Sole Cutlets

Prep time: 15 minutes | Cook time: 10 minutes | Serves 2

1 egg	taste
120 g Pecorino Romano cheese, grated	½ teaspoon cayenne pepper
Sea salt and white pepper, to	1 teaspoon dried parsley flakes
	2 sole fillets

1. To make a breading station, whisk the egg until frothy. 2. In another bowl, mix Pecorino Romano cheese, and spices. 3. Dip the fish in the egg mixture and turn to coat evenly; then, dredge in the cracker crumb mixture, turning a couple of times to coat evenly. 4. Cook in the preheated air fryer at 200ºC for 5 minutes; turn them over and cook another 5 minutes. Enjoy!

Parmesan-Crusted Hake with Garlic Sauce

Prep time: 5 minutes | Cook time: 10 minutes | Serves 3

Fish:	3 hake fillets, patted dry
6 tablespoons mayonnaise	Nonstick cooking spray
1 tablespoon fresh lime juice	Garlic Sauce:
1 teaspoon Dijon mustard	60 ml plain Greek yogurt
150 g grated Parmesan cheese	2 tablespoons olive oil
Salt, to taste	2 cloves garlic, minced
¼ teaspoon ground black pepper, or more to taste	½ teaspoon minced tarragon leaves

1. Preheat the air fryer to 200ºC. 2. Mix the mayo, lime juice, and mustard in a shallow bowl and whisk to combine. In another shallow bowl, stir together the grated Parmesan cheese, salt, and pepper. 3. Dredge each fillet in the mayo mixture, then roll them in the cheese mixture until they are evenly coated on both sides. 4. Spray the air fryer basket with nonstick cooking spray. Arrange the fillets in the basket and air fry for 10 minutes, or until the fish flakes easily with a fork. Flip the fillets halfway through the cooking time. 5. Meanwhile, in a small bowl, whisk all the ingredients for the sauce until well incorporated. 6. Serve the fish warm alongside the sauce.

Quick Prawns Skewers

Prep time: 10 minutes | Cook time: 5 minutes | Serves 5

1.8kg prawns, peeled and deveined	1 tablespoon avocado oil
1 tablespoon dried rosemary	1 teaspoon apple cider vinegar

1. Mix the prawns with dried rosemary, avocado oil, and apple cider vinegar. 2. Then thread the prawns onto skewers and put in the air fryer. 3. Cook the prawns at 200ºC for 5 minutes.

Tuna Patty Sliders

Prep time: 15 minutes | Cook time: 10 to 15 minutes | Serves 4

3 cans tuna, 140 g each, packed in water	1 tablespoon Sriracha
40 g whole-wheat panko bread crumbs	¾ teaspoon black pepper
50 g shredded Parmesan cheese	10 whole-wheat buns
	Cooking spray

1. Preheat the air fryer to 175ºC. 2. Spray the air fryer basket lightly with cooking spray. 3. In a medium bowl combine the tuna, bread crumbs, Parmesan cheese, Sriracha, and black pepper and stir to combine. 4. Form the mixture into 10 patties. 5. Place the patties in the air fryer basket in a single layer. Spray the patties lightly with cooking spray. You may need to cook them in batches. 6. Air fry for 6 to 8 minutes. Turn the patties over and lightly spray with cooking spray. Air fry until golden brown and crisp, another 4 to 7 more minutes. Serve warm.

Blackened Red Snapper

Prep time: 13 minutes | Cook time: 8 to 10 minutes | Serves 4

1½ teaspoons black pepper	4 red snapper fillet portions, skin on, 110 g each
¼ teaspoon thyme	4 thin slices lemon
¼ teaspoon garlic powder	Cooking spray
⅛ teaspoon cayenne pepper	
1 teaspoon olive oil	

1. Mix the spices and oil together to make a paste. Rub into both sides of the fish. 2. Spray the air fryer basket with nonstick cooking spray and lay snapper steaks in basket, skin-side down. 3. Place a lemon slice on each piece of fish. 4. Roast at 200ºC for 8 to 10 minutes. The fish will not flake when done, but it should be white through the center.

Chapter 7 Beef, Pork, and Lamb

Chapter 7 Beef, Pork, and Lamb

Pork Bulgogi

Prep time: 30 minutes | Cook time: 15 minutes | Serves 4

1 onion, thinly sliced
2 tablespoons gochujang (Korean red chili paste)
1 tablespoon minced fresh ginger
1 tablespoon minced garlic
1 tablespoon soy sauce
1 tablespoon Shaoxing wine (rice cooking wine)
1 tablespoon toasted sesame oil

1 teaspoon sugar
¼ to 1 teaspoon cayenne pepper or gochugaru (Korean ground red pepper)
450 g boneless pork shoulder, cut into ½-inch-thick slices
1 tablespoon sesame seeds
60 ml sliced spring onionspring onions

1. In a large bowl, combine the onion, gochujang, ginger, garlic, soy sauce, wine, sesame oil, sugar, and cayenne. Add the pork and toss to coat. Marinate at room temperature for 30 minutes, or cover and refrigerate for up to 24 hours. 2. Arrange the pork and onion slices in the air fryer basket; discard the marinade. Set the air fryer to 200ºC for 15 minutes, turning the pork halfway through the cooking time. 3. Arrange the pork on a serving platter. Sprinkle with the sesame seeds and spring onionspring onions and serve.

Cheesy Low-Carb Lasagna

Prep time: 10 minutes | Cook time: 10 minutes | Serves 4

Meat Layer:
Extra-virgin olive oil
450 g 85% lean beef mince
235 ml marinara sauce
60 ml diced celery
60 ml diced red onion
½ teaspoon minced garlic
Coarse or flaky salt and black pepper, to taste
Cheese Layer:

230 g ricotta cheese
235 ml shredded Mozzarella cheese
120 ml grated Parmesan cheese
2 large eggs
1 teaspoon dried Italian seasoning, crushed
½ teaspoon each minced garlic, garlic powder, and black pepper

1. For the meat layer: Grease a cake pan with 1 teaspoon olive oil. 2. In a large bowl, combine the beef mince, marinara, celery, onion, garlic, salt, and pepper. Place the seasoned meat in the pan. 3. Place the pan in the air fryer basket. Set the air fryer to 190ºC for 10 minutes. 4. Meanwhile, for the cheese layer: In a medium bowl, combine the ricotta, half the Mozzarella, the Parmesan, lightly beaten eggs, Italian seasoning, minced garlic, garlic powder, and

pepper. Stir until well blended. 5. At the end of the cooking time, spread the cheese mixture over the meat mixture. Sprinkle with the remaining 120 ml Mozzarella. Set the air fryer to 190ºC for 10 minutes, or until the cheese is browned and bubbling. 6. At the end of the cooking time, use a meat thermometer to ensure the meat has reached an internal temperature of 70ºC. 7. Drain the fat and liquid from the pan. Let stand for 5 minutes before serving.

Smoky Pork Tenderloin

Prep time: 5 minutes | Cook time: 19 to 22 minutes | Serves 6

680 g pork tenderloin
1 tablespoon avocado oil
1 teaspoon chili powder
1 teaspoon smoked paprika

1 teaspoon garlic powder
1 teaspoon sea salt
1 teaspoon freshly ground black pepper

1. Pierce the tenderloin all over with a fork and rub the oil all over the meat. 2. In a small dish, stir together the chili powder, smoked paprika, garlic powder, salt, and pepper. 3. Rub the spice mixture all over the tenderloin. 4. Set the air fryer to 200ºC. Place the pork in the air fryer basket and air fry for 10 minutes. Flip the tenderloin and cook for 9 to 12 minutes more, until an instant-read thermometer reads at least 65ºC. 5. Allow the tenderloin to rest for 5 minutes, then slice and serve.

Chinese-Style Baby Back Ribs

Prep time: 30 minutes | Cook time: 30 minutes | Serves 4

1 tablespoon toasted sesame oil
1 tablespoon fermented black bean paste
1 tablespoon Shaoxing wine (rice cooking wine)
1 tablespoon dark soy sauce

1 tablespoon agave nectar or honey
1 teaspoon minced garlic
1 teaspoon minced fresh ginger
1 (680 g) slab baby back ribs, cut into individual ribs

1. In a large bowl, stir together the sesame oil, black bean paste, wine, soy sauce, agave, garlic, and ginger. Add the ribs and toss well to coat. Marinate at room temperature for 30 minutes, or cover and refrigerate for up to 24 hours. 2. Place the ribs in the air fryer basket; discard the marinade. Set the air fryer to 175ºC for 30 minutes.

German Rouladen-Style Steak

Prep time: 20 minutes | Cook time: 15 minutes | Serves 4

Onion Sauce:
2 medium onions, cut into
½-inch-thick slices
Coarse or flaky salt and black
pepper, to taste
120 ml sour cream
1 tablespoon tomato paste
2 teaspoons chopped fresh

parsley
Rouladen:
60 ml Dijon mustard
450 g bavette or skirt steak, ¼
to ½ inch thick
1 teaspoon black pepper
4 slices bacon
60 ml chopped fresh parsley

1. For the sauce: In a small bowl, mix together the onions with salt and pepper to taste. Place the onions in the air fryer basket. Set the air fryer to 200°C for 6 minutes, or until the onions are softened and golden brown. 2. Set aside half of the onions to use in the rouladen. Place the rest in a small bowl and add the sour cream, tomato paste, parsley, ½ teaspoon salt, and ½ teaspoon pepper. Stir until well combined, adding 1 to 2 tablespoons of water, if necessary, to thin the sauce slightly. Set the sauce aside. 3. For the rouladen: Evenly spread the mustard over the meat. Sprinkle with the pepper. Top with the bacon slices, reserved onions, and parsley. Starting at the long end, roll up the steak as tightly as possible, ending seam side down. Use 2 or 3 wooden toothpicks to hold the roll together. Using a sharp knife, cut the roll in half so that it better fits in the air fryer basket. 4. Place the steak, seam side down, in the air fryer basket. Set the air fryer to 200°C for 9 minutes. Use a meat thermometer to ensure the steak has reached an internal temperature of 65°C. (It is critical to not overcook bavette steak, so as to not toughen the meat.) 5. Let the steak rest for 10 minutes before cutting into slices. Serve with the sauce.

Sausage and Peppers

Prep time: 7 minutes | Cook time: 35 minutes | Serves 4

Oil, for spraying
900 g hot or sweet Italian-
seasoned sausage links, cut into
thick slices
4 large peppers of any color,
seeded and cut into slices
1 onion, thinly sliced

1 tablespoon olive oil
1 tablespoon chopped fresh
parsley
1 teaspoon dried oregano
1 teaspoon dried basil
1 teaspoon balsamic vinegar

1. Line the air fryer basket with parchment and spray lightly with oil. 2. In a large bowl, combine the sausage, peppers, and onion. 3. In a small bowl, whisk together the olive oil, parsley, oregano, basil, and balsamic vinegar. Pour the mixture over the sausage and peppers and toss until evenly coated. 4. Using a slotted spoon, transfer the mixture to the prepared basket, taking care to drain out as much excess liquid as possible. 5. Air fry at 175°C for 20 minutes, stir, and cook for another 15 minutes, or until the sausage is browned and the juices run clear.

Spicy Bavette Steak with Zhoug

Prep time: 30 minutes | Cook time: 8 minutes | Serves 4

Marinade and Steak:
120 ml dark beer or orange
juice
60 ml fresh lemon juice
3 cloves garlic, minced
2 tablespoons extra-virgin olive
oil
2 tablespoons Sriracha
2 tablespoons brown sugar
2 teaspoons ground cumin
2 teaspoons smoked paprika
1 tablespoon coarse or flaky salt
1 teaspoon black pepper

680 g bavette or skirt steak,
trimmed and cut into 3 pieces
Zhoug:
235 ml packed fresh coriander
leaves
2 cloves garlic, peeled
2 jalapeño or green chiles,
stemmed and coarsely chopped
½ teaspoon ground cumin
¼ teaspoon ground coriander
¼ teaspoon coarse or flaky salt
2 to 4 tablespoons extra-virgin
olive oil

1. For the marinade and steak: In a small bowl, whisk together the beer, lemon juice, garlic, olive oil, Sriracha, brown sugar, cumin, paprika, salt, and pepper. Place the steak in a large resealable plastic bag. Pour the marinade over the steak, seal the bag, and massage the steak to coat. Marinate in the refrigerator for 1 hour or up to 24 hours, turning the bag occasionally. 2. Meanwhile, for the zhoug: In a food processor, combine the coriander, garlic, jalapeños, cumin, coriander, and salt. Process until finely chopped. Add 2 tablespoons olive oil and pulse to form a loose paste, adding up to 2 tablespoons more olive oil if needed. Transfer the zhoug to a glass container. Cover and store in the refrigerator until 30 minutes before serving if marinating more than 1 hour. 3. Remove the steak from the marinade and discard the marinade. Place the steak in the air fryer basket and set the air fryer to 200°C for 8 minutes. Use a meat thermometer to ensure the steak has reached an internal temperature of 65°C (for medium). 4. Transfer the steak to a cutting board and let rest for 5 minutes. Slice the steak across the grain and serve with the zhoug.

Mustard Herb Pork Tenderloin

Prep time: 5 minutes | Cook time: 20 minutes | Serves 6

60 ml mayonnaise
2 tablespoons Dijon mustard
½ teaspoon dried thyme
¼ teaspoon dried rosemary

1 (450 g) pork tenderloin
½ teaspoon salt
¼ teaspoon ground black
pepper

1. In a small bowl, mix mayonnaise, mustard, thyme, and rosemary. Brush tenderloin with mixture on all sides, then sprinkle with salt and pepper on all sides. 2. Place tenderloin into ungreased air fryer basket. Adjust the temperature to 200°C and air fry for 20 minutes, turning tenderloin halfway through cooking. Tenderloin will be golden and have an internal temperature of at least 65°C when done. Serve warm.

Sweet and Spicy Country-Style Ribs

Prep time: 10 minutes | Cook time: 25 minutes | Serves 4

2 tablespoons brown sugar	1 teaspoon coarse or flaky salt
2 tablespoons smoked paprika	1 teaspoon black pepper
1 teaspoon garlic powder	¼ to ½ teaspoon cayenne
1 teaspoon onion granules	pepper
1 teaspoon mustard powder	680 g boneless pork steaks
1 teaspoon ground cumin	235 ml barbecue sauce

1. In a small bowl, stir together the brown sugar, paprika, garlic powder, onion granules, mustard powder, cumin, salt, black pepper, and cayenne. Mix until well combined. 2. Pat the ribs dry with a paper towel. Generously sprinkle the rub evenly over both sides of the ribs and rub in with your fingers. 3. Place the ribs in the air fryer basket. Set the air fryer to 175ºC for 15 minutes. Turn the ribs and brush with 120 ml of the barbecue sauce. Cook for an additional 10 minutes. Use a meat thermometer to ensure the pork has reached an internal temperature of 65ºC. 4. Serve with remaining barbecue sauce.

Pork Schnitzel with Dill Sauce

Prep time: 5 minutes | Cook time: 24 minutes | Serves 4 to 6

6 bonelesspork chops (about 680 g)	3 tablespoons butter, melted
120 ml flour	2 tablespoons vegetable or olive oil
1½ teaspoons salt	lemon wedges
Freshly ground black pepper, to taste	Dill Sauce:
2 eggs	235 ml chicken stock
120 ml milk	1½ tablespoons cornflour
355 ml toasted fine bread crumbs	80 ml sour cream
1 teaspoon paprika	1½ tablespoons chopped fresh dill
	Salt and pepper, to taste

1. Trim the excess fat from the pork chops and pound each chop with a meat mallet between two pieces of plastic wrap until they are ½-inch thick. 2. Set up a dredging station. Combine the flour, salt, and black pepper in a shallow dish. Whisk the eggs and milk together in a second shallow dish. Finally, combine the bread crumbs and paprika in a third shallow dish. 3. Dip each flattened pork chop in the flour. Shake off the excess flour and dip each chop into the egg mixture. Finally dip them into the bread crumbs and press the bread crumbs onto the meat firmly. Place each finished chop on a baking sheet until they are all coated. 4. Preheat the air fryer to 200ºC. 5. Combine the melted butter and the oil in a small bowl and lightly brush both sides of the coated pork chops. Do not brush the chops too heavily or the breading will not be as crispy. 6. Air fry one schnitzel at a time for 4 minutes, turning it over halfway through the cooking time. Hold the cooked schnitzels warm on a baking pan in a 75ºC oven while you finish air frying the rest. 7. While the schnitzels are cooking, whisk the chicken stock and cornflour together in a small saucepan over medium-high heat on the stovetop. Bring the mixture to a boil and simmer for 2 minutes. Remove the saucepan from heat and whisk in the sour cream. Add the chopped fresh dill and season with salt and pepper. 8. Transfer the pork schnitzel to a platter and serve with dill sauce and lemon wedges.

Sumptuous Pizza Tortilla Rolls

Prep time: 10 minutes | Cook time: 6 minutes | Serves 4

1 teaspoon butter	8 flour tortillas
½ medium onion, slivered	8 thin slices wafer-thinham
½ red or green pepper, julienned	24 pepperoni slices
110 g fresh white mushrooms, chopped	235 ml shredded Mozzarella cheese
120 ml pizza sauce	Cooking spray

1. Preheat the air fryer to 200ºC. 2. Put butter, onions, pepper, and mushrooms in a baking pan. Bake in the preheated air fryer for 3 minutes. Stir and cook 3 to 4 minutes longer until just crisp and tender. Remove pan and set aside. 3. To assemble rolls, spread about 2 teaspoons of pizza sauce on one half of each tortilla. Top with a slice of ham and 3 slices of pepperoni. Divide sautéed vegetables among tortillas and top with cheese. 4. Roll up tortillas, secure with toothpicks if needed, and spray with oil. 5. Put 4 rolls in air fryer basket and air fry for 4 minutes. Turn and air fry 4 minutes, until heated through and lightly browned. 6. Repeat step 4 to air fry remaining pizza rolls. 7. Serve immediately.

Rosemary Ribeye Steaks

Prep time: 10 minutes | Cook time: 15 minutes | Serves 2

60 ml butter	1½ tablespoons balsamic
1 clove garlic, minced	vinegar
Salt and ground black pepper, to taste	60 ml rosemary, chopped
	2 ribeye steaks

1. Melt the butter in a skillet over medium heat. Add the garlic and fry until fragrant. 2. Remove the skillet from the heat and add the salt, pepper, and vinegar. Allow it to cool. 3. Add the rosemary, then pour the mixture into a Ziploc bag. 4. Put the ribeye steaks in the bag and shake well, coating the meat well. Refrigerate for an hour, then allow to sit for a further twenty minutes. 5. Preheat the air fryer to 200ºC. 6. Air fry the ribeye steaks for 15 minutes. 7. Take care when removing the steaks from the air fryer and plate up. 8. Serve immediately.

Italian Lamb Chops with Avocado Mayo

Prep time: 5 minutes | Cook time: 12 minutes | Serves 2

2 lamp chops
2 teaspoons Italian herbs
2 avocados
120 ml mayonnaise
1 tablespoon lemon juice

1. Season the lamb chops with the Italian herbs, then set aside for 5 minutes. 2. Preheat the air fryer to 200ºC and place the rack inside. 3. Put the chops on the rack and air fry for 12 minutes. 4. In the meantime, halve the avocados and open to remove the pits. Spoon the flesh into a blender. 5. Add the mayonnaise and lemon juice and pulse until a smooth consistency is achieved. 6. Take care when removing the chops from the air fryer, then plate up and serve with the avocado mayo.

Vietnamese "Shaking" Beef

Prep time: 30 minutes | Cook time: 4 minutes per batch | Serves 4

Meat:
4 garlic cloves, minced
2 teaspoons soy sauce
2 teaspoons sugar
1 teaspoon toasted sesame oil
1 teaspoon coarse or flaky salt
¼ teaspoon black pepper
680 g flat iron or top rump steak, cut into 1-inch cubes
Salad:
2 tablespoons rice vinegar or apple cider vinegar
2 tablespoons vegetable oil
1 garlic clove, minced
2 teaspoons sugar
¼ teaspoon coarse or flaky salt
¼ teaspoon black pepper
½ red onion, halved and very thinly sliced
1 head butterhead lettuce, leaves separated and torn into large pieces
120 ml halved baby plum tomatoes
60 ml fresh mint leaves
For Serving:
Lime wedges
Coarse salt and freshly cracked black pepper, to taste

1. For the meat: In a small bowl, combine the garlic, soy sauce, sugar, sesame oil, salt, and pepper. Place the meat in a gallon-size resealable plastic bag. Pour the marinade over the meat. Seal and place the bag in a large bowl. Marinate for 30 minutes, or cover and refrigerate for up to 24 hours. 2. Place half the meat in the air fryer basket. Set the air fryer to 230ºC for 4 minutes, shaking the basket to redistribute the meat halfway through the cooking time. Transfer the meat to a plate (it should be medium-rare, still pink in the middle). Cover lightly with aluminum foil. Repeat to cook the remaining meat. 3. Meanwhile, for the salad: In a large bowl, whisk together the vinegar, vegetable oil, garlic, sugar, salt, and pepper. Add the onion. Stir to combine. Add the lettuce, tomatoes, and mint and toss to combine. Arrange the salad on a serving platter. 4. Arrange the cooked meat over the salad. Drizzle any accumulated juices from the plate over the meat. Serve with lime wedges, coarse salt, and cracked black pepper.

Bacon-Wrapped Cheese Pork

Prep time: 10 minutes | Cook time: 20 minutes | Serves 4

4 (1-inch-thick) boneless pork chops
2 (150 g) packages Boursin
cheese
8 slices thin-cut bacon

1. Spray the air fryer basket with avocado oil. Preheat the air fryer to 200ºC. 2. Place one of the chops on a cutting board. With a sharp knife held parallel to the cutting board, make a 1-inch-wide incision on the top edge of the chop. Carefully cut into the chop to form a large pocket, leaving a ½-inch border along the sides and bottom. Repeat with the other 3 chops. 3. Snip the corner of a large resealable plastic bag to form a ¾-inch hole. Place the Boursin cheese in the bag and pipe the cheese into the pockets in the chops, dividing the cheese evenly among them. 4. Wrap 2 slices of bacon around each chop and secure the ends with toothpicks. Place the bacon-wrapped chops in the air fryer basket and cook for 10 minutes, then flip the chops and cook for another 8 to 10 minutes, until the bacon is crisp, the chops are cooked through, and the internal temperature reaches 65ºC. 5. Store leftovers in an airtight container in the refrigerator for up to 3 days. Reheat in a preheated 200ºC air fryer for 5 minutes, or until warmed through.

Greek Lamb Pitta Pockets

Prep time: 15 minutes | Cook time: 6 minutes | Serves 4

Dressing:
235 ml plain yogurt
1 tablespoon lemon juice
1 teaspoon dried dill, crushed
1 teaspoon ground oregano
½ teaspoon salt
Meatballs:
230 g lamb mince
1 tablespoon diced onion
1 teaspoon dried parsley
1 teaspoon dried dill, crushed
¼ teaspoon oregano
¼ teaspoon coriander
¼ teaspoon ground cumin
¼ teaspoon salt
4 pitta halves
Suggested Toppings:
1 red onion, slivered
1 medium cucumber, deseeded, thinly sliced
Crumbled feta cheese
Sliced black olives
Chopped fresh peppers

1. Preheat the air fryer to 200ºC. 2. Stir the dressing ingredients together in a small bowl and refrigerate while preparing lamb. 3. Combine all meatball ingredients in a large bowl and stir to distribute seasonings. 4. Shape meat mixture into 12 small meatballs, rounded or slightly flattened if you prefer. 5. Transfer the meatballs in the preheated air fryer and air fry for 6 minutes, until well done. Remove and drain on paper towels. 6. To serve, pile meatballs and the choice of toppings in pitta pockets and drizzle with dressing.

Beef Burger

Prep time: 20 minutes | Cook time: 12 minutes | Serves 4

570 g lean beef mince	½ teaspoon cumin powder
1 tablespoon soy sauce or tamari	60 ml spring onions, minced
1 teaspoon Dijon mustard	⅓ teaspoon sea salt flakes
1/2 teaspoon smoked paprika	⅓ teaspoon freshly cracked mixed peppercorns
1 teaspoon shallot powder	1 teaspoon celery salt
1 clove garlic, minced	1 teaspoon dried parsley

1. Mix all of the above ingredients in a bowl; knead until everything is well incorporated. 2. Shape the mixture into four patties. Next, make a shallow dip in the center of each patty to prevent them puffing up during air frying. 3. Spritz the patties on all sides using nonstick cooking spray. Cook approximately 12 minutes at 180°C. 4. Check for doneness, an instant-read thermometer should read 70°C. Bon appétit!

Deconstructed Chicago Dogs

Prep time: 10 minutes | Cook time: 7 minutes | Serves 4

4 hot dogs	peppers, diced
2 large dill pickles	For Garnish (Optional):
60 ml diced onions	Wholegrain or Dijon mustard
1 tomato, cut into ½-inch dice	Celery salt
4 pickled or brined jalapeno	Poppy seeds

1. Spray the air fryer basket with avocado oil. Preheat the air fryer to 200°C. 2. Place the hot dogs in the air fryer basket and air fry for 5 to 7 minutes, until hot and slightly crispy. 3. While the hot dogs cook, quarter one of the dill pickles lengthwise, so that you have 4 pickle spears. Finely dice the other pickle. 4. When the hot dogs are done, transfer them to a serving platter and arrange them in a row, alternating with the pickle spears. Top with the diced pickles, onions, tomato, and jalapeno peppers. Drizzle mustard on top and garnish with celery salt and poppy seeds, if desired. 5. Best served fresh. Store leftover hot dogs in an airtight container in the refrigerator for up to 3 days. Reheat in a preheated 200°C air fryer for 2 minutes, or until warmed through.

Cheese Wine Pork Loin

Prep time: 30 minutes | Cook time: 15 minutes | Serves 2

235 ml water	1 teaspoon onion granules
235 ml red wine	½ teaspoon porcini powder
1 tablespoon sea salt	Sea salt and ground black pepper, to taste
2 pork loin steaks	
60 ml ground almonds	1 egg
60 ml flaxseed meal	60 ml yoghurt
½ teaspoon baking powder	1 teaspoon wholegrain or

English mustard	80 ml Parmesan cheese, grated

1. In a large ceramic dish, combine the water, wine and salt. Add the pork and put for 1 hour in the refrigerator. 2. In a shallow bowl, mix the ground almonds, flaxseed meal, baking powder, onion granules, porcini powder, salt, and ground pepper. In another bowl, whisk the eggs with yoghurt and mustard. 3. In a third bowl, place the grated Parmesan cheese. 4. Dip the pork in the seasoned flour mixture and toss evenly; then, in the egg mixture. Finally, roll them over the grated Parmesan cheese. 5. Spritz the bottom of the air fryer basket with cooking oil. Add the breaded pork and cook at 200°C and for 10 minutes. 6. Flip and cook for 5 minutes more on the other side. Serve warm.

Panko Crusted Calf's Liver Strips

Prep time: 15 minutes | Cook time: 23 to 25 minutes | Serves 4

450 g sliced calf's liver, cut into ½-inch wide strips	475 ml panko breadcrumbs
	Salt and ground black pepper, to taste
2 eggs	
2 tablespoons milk	Cooking spray
120 ml whole wheat flour	

1. Preheat the air fryer to 200°C and spritz with cooking spray. 2. Rub the calf's liver strips with salt and ground black pepper on a clean work surface. 3. Whisk the eggs with milk in a large bowl. Pour the flour in a shallow dish. Pour the panko on a separate shallow dish. 4. Dunk the liver strips in the flour, then in the egg mixture. Shake the excess off and roll the strips over the panko to coat well. 5. Arrange half of the liver strips in a single layer in the preheated air fryer and spritz with cooking spray. 6. Air fry for 5 minutes or until browned. Flip the strips halfway through. Repeat with the remaining strips. 7. Serve immediately.

Beef and Spinach Rolls

Prep time: 10 minutes | Cook time: 14 minutes | Serves 2

3 teaspoons pesto	85 g roasted red peppers
900 g beef bavette or skirt steak	180 ml baby spinach
6 slices low-moisture Mozarella or other melting cheese	1 teaspoon sea salt
	1 teaspoon black pepper

1. Preheat the air fryer to 200°C. 2. Spoon equal amounts of the pesto onto each steak and spread it across evenly. 3. Put the cheese, roasted red peppers and spinach on top of the meat, about three-quarters of the way down. 4. Roll the steak up, holding it in place with toothpicks. Sprinkle with the sea salt and pepper. 5. Put inside the air fryer and air fry for 14 minutes, turning halfway through the cooking time. 6. Allow the beef to rest for 10 minutes before slicing up and serving.

Spicy Rump Steak

Prep time: 25 minutes | Cook time: 12 to 18 minutes | Serves 4

2 tablespoons salsa	black pepper
1 tablespoon minced chipotle pepper or chipotle paste	⅛ teaspoon red pepper flakes
1 tablespoon apple cider vinegar	340 g rump steak, cut into 4 pieces and gently pounded to about ⅓ inch thick
1 teaspoon ground cumin	Cooking oil spray
⅛ teaspoon freshly ground	

1. In a small bowl, thoroughly mix the salsa, chipotle pepper, vinegar, cumin, black pepper, and red pepper flakes. Rub this mixture into both sides of each steak piece. Let stand for 15 minutes at room temperature. 2. Insert the crisper plate into the basket and place the basket into the unit. Preheat the unit by selecting AIR FRY, setting the temperature to 200ºC, and setting the time to 3 minutes. Select START/STOP to begin. 3. Once the unit is preheated, spray the crisper plate with cooking oil. Working in batches, place 2 steaks into the basket. 4. Select AIR FRY, set the temperature to 200ºC, and set the time to 9 minutes. Select START/STOP to begin. 5. After about 6 minutes, check the steaks. If a food thermometer inserted into the meat registers at least 65ºC, they are done. If not, resume cooking. 6. When the cooking is done, transfer the steaks to a clean plate and cover with aluminum foil to keep warm. Repeat steps 3, 4, and 5 with the remaining steaks. 7. Thinly slice the steaks against the grain and serve.

Teriyaki Rump Steak with Broccoli and Capsicum

Prep time: 5 minutes | Cook time: 13 minutes | Serves 4

230 g rump steak	2 red peppers, sliced
80 ml teriyaki marinade	Fine sea salt and ground black pepper, to taste
1½ teaspoons sesame oil	Cooking spray
½ head broccoli, cut into florets	

1. Toss the rump steak in a large bowl with teriyaki marinade. Wrap the bowl in plastic and refrigerate to marinate for at least an hour. 2. Preheat the air fryer to 200ºC and spritz with cooking spray. 3. Discard the marinade and transfer the steak in the preheated air fryer. Spritz with cooking spray. 4. Air fry for 13 minutes or until well browned. Flip the steak halfway through. 5. Meanwhile, heat the sesame oil in a nonstick skillet over medium heat. Add the broccoli and red pepper. Sprinkle with salt and ground black pepper. Sauté for 5 minutes or until the broccoli is tender. 6. Transfer the air fried rump steak on a plate and top with the sautéed broccoli and pepper. Serve hot.

Pork Chops with Caramelized Onions

Prep time: 20 minutes | Cook time: 23 to 34 minutes | Serves 4

4 bone-in pork chops (230 g each)	divided
1 to 2 tablespoons oil	1 brown onion, thinly sliced
2 tablespoons Cajun seasoning,	1 green pepper, thinly sliced
	2 tablespoons light brown sugar

1. Spritz the pork chops with oil. Sprinkle 1 tablespoon of Cajun seasoning on one side of the chops. 2. Preheat the air fryer to 200ºC. Line the air fryer basket with parchment paper and spritz the parchment with oil. 3. Place 2 pork chops, spice-side up, on the paper. 4. Cook for 4 minutes. Flip the chops, sprinkle with the remaining 1 tablespoon of Cajun seasoning, and cook for 4 to 8 minutes more until the internal temperature reaches 65ºC, depending on the chops' thickness. Remove and keep warm while you cook the remaining 2 chops. Set the chops aside. 5. In a baking pan, combine the onion, pepper, and brown sugar, stirring until the vegetables are coated. Place the pan in the air fryer basket and cook for 4 minutes. 6. Stir the vegetables. Cook for 3 to 6 minutes more to your desired doneness. Spoon the vegetable mixture over the chops to serve.

Spicy Lamb Sirloin Chops

Prep time: 30 minutes | Cook time: 15 minutes | Serves 4

½ brown onion, coarsely chopped	1 teaspoon ground cinnamon
4 coin-size slices peeled fresh ginger	1 teaspoon ground turmeric
	½ to 1 teaspoon cayenne pepper
5 garlic cloves	½ teaspoon ground cardamom
1 teaspoon garam masala	1 teaspoon coarse or flaky salt
1 teaspoon ground fennel	450 g lamb sirloin chops

1. In a blender, combine the onion, ginger, garlic, garam masala, fennel, cinnamon, turmeric, cayenne, cardamom, and salt. Pulse until the onion is finely minced and the mixture forms a thick paste, 3 to 4 minutes. 2. Place the lamb chops in a large bowl. Slash the meat and fat with a sharp knife several times to allow the marinade to penetrate better. Add the spice paste to the bowl and toss the lamb to coat. Marinate at room temperature for 30 minutes or cover and refrigerate for up to 24 hours. 3. Place the lamb chops in a single layer in the air fryer basket. Set the air fryer to 165ºC for 15 minutes, turning the chops halfway through the cooking time. Use a meat thermometer to ensure the lamb has reached an internal temperature of 65ºC (medium-rare).

Macadamia Nuts Crusted Pork Rack

Prep time: 5 minutes | Cook time: 35 minutes | Serves 2

1 clove garlic, minced	1 tablespoon breadcrumbs
2 tablespoons olive oil	1 tablespoon rosemary, chopped
450 g rack of pork	1 egg
235 ml chopped macadamia nuts	Salt and ground black pepper, to taste

1. Preheat the air fryer to 175ºC. 2. Combine the garlic and olive oil in a small bowl. Stir to mix well. 3. On a clean work surface, rub the pork rack with the garlic oil and sprinkle with salt and black pepper on both sides. 4. Combine the macadamia nuts, breadcrumbs, and rosemary in a shallow dish. Whisk the egg in a large bowl. 5. Dredge the pork in the egg, then roll the pork over the macadamia nut mixture to coat well. Shake the excess off. 6. Arrange the pork in the preheated air fryer and air fry for 30 minutes on both sides. Increase to 200ºC and fry for 5 more minutes or until the pork is well browned. 7. Serve immediately.

Pork Medallions with Endive Salad

Prep time: 25 minutes | Cook time: 7 minutes | Serves 4

1 (230 g) pork tenderloin	honey or maple syrup)
Salt and freshly ground black pepper, to taste	1 tablespoon Dijon mustard
60 ml flour	juice of ½ lemon
2 eggs, lightly beaten	2 tablespoons chopped chervil or flat-leaf parsley
180 ml finely crushed crackers	salt and freshly ground black pepper
1 teaspoon paprika	120 ml extra-virgin olive oil
1 teaspoon mustard powder	Endive Salad:
1 teaspoon garlic powder	1 heart romaine lettuce, torn into large pieces
1 teaspoon dried thyme	2 heads endive, sliced
1 teaspoon salt	120 ml cherry tomatoes, halved
vegetable or rapeseed oil, in spray bottle	85 g fresh Mozzarella, diced
Vinaigrette:	Salt and freshly ground black pepper, to taste
60 ml white balsamic vinegar	
2 tablespoons agave syrup (or	

1. Slice the pork tenderloin into 1-inch slices. Using a meat pounder, pound the pork slices into thin ½-inch medallions. Generously season the pork with salt and freshly ground black pepper on both sides. 2. Set up a dredging station using three shallow dishes. Put the flour in one dish and the beaten eggs in a second dish. Combine the crushed crackers, paprika, mustard powder, garlic powder, thyme and salt in a third dish. 3. Preheat the air fryer to 200ºC. 4. Dredge the pork medallions in flour first and then into the beaten egg. Let the excess egg drip off and coat both sides of the medallions with the cracker crumb mixture. Spray both sides of the coated medallions with vegetable or rapeseed oil. 5. Air fry the medallions in two batches at 200ºC for 5 minutes. Once you have air-fried all the medallions, flip them all over and return the first batch of medallions back into the air fryer on top of the second batch. Air fry at 200ºC for an additional 2 minutes. 6. While the medallions are cooking, make the salad and dressing. Whisk the white balsamic vinegar, agave syrup, Dijon mustard, lemon juice, chervil, salt and pepper together in a small bowl. Whisk in the olive oil slowly until combined and thickened. 7. Combine the romaine lettuce, endive, cherry tomatoes, and Mozzarella cheese in a large salad bowl. Drizzle the dressing over the vegetables and toss to combine. Season with salt and freshly ground black pepper. 8. Serve the pork medallions warm on or beside the salad.

Indian Mint and Chile Kebabs

Prep time: 30 minutes | Cook time: 15 minutes | Serves 4

450 g lamb mince	½ teaspoon ground turmeric
120 ml finely minced onion	½ teaspoon cayenne pepper
60 ml chopped fresh mint	¼ teaspoon ground cardamom
60 ml chopped fresh coriander	¼ teaspoon ground cinnamon
1 tablespoon minced garlic	1 teaspoon coarse or flaky salt

1. In the bowl of a stand mixer fitted with the paddle attachment, combine the lamb, onion, mint, coriander, garlic, turmeric, cayenne, cardamom, cinnamon, and salt. Mix on low speed until you have a sticky mess of spiced meat. If you have time, let the mixture stand at room temperature for 30 minutes (or cover and refrigerate for up to a day or two, until you're ready to make the kebabs). 2. Divide the meat into eight equal portions. Form each into a long sausage shape. Place the kebabs in a single layer in the air fryer basket. Set the air fryer to 175ºC for 10 minutes. Increase the air fryer temperature to 200ºC and cook for 3 to 4 minutes more to brown the kebabs. Use a meat thermometer to ensure the kebabs have reached an internal temperature of 70ºC (medium).

Beef Whirls

Prep time: 30 minutes | Cook time: 18 minutes | Serves 6

3 minute steaks (170 g each)	1 teaspoon dried basil
1 (450 g) bottle Italian dressing	1 teaspoon dried oregano
235 ml Italian-style bread crumbs (or plain bread crumbs with Italian seasoning to taste)	1 teaspoon dried parsley
	60 ml beef stock
	1 to 2 tablespoons oil
120 ml grated Parmesan cheese	

1. In a large resealable bag, combine the steaks and Italian dressing. Seal the bag and refrigerate to marinate for 2 hours. 2. In a medium bowl, whisk the bread crumbs, cheese, basil, oregano, and parsley until blended. Stir in the beef stock. 3. Place the steaks on a cutting board and cut each in half so you have 6 equal pieces. Sprinkle with the bread crumb mixture. Roll up the steaks, jelly roll-style, and secure with toothpicks. 4. Preheat the air fryer to 200ºC. 5. Place 3 roll-ups in the air fryer basket. 6. Cook for 5 minutes. Flip the roll-ups and spritz with oil. Cook for 4 minutes more until the internal temperature reaches 65ºC. Repeat with the remaining roll-ups. Let rest for 5 to 10 minutes before serving.

Tomato and Bacon Zoodles

Prep time: 10 minutes | Cook time: 15 to 22 minutes | Serves 2

230 g sliced bacon
120 ml baby plum tomatoes
1 large courgette, spiralized
120 ml ricotta cheese

60 ml double/whipping cream
80 ml finely grated Parmesan cheese, plus more for serving
Sea salt and freshly ground black pepper, to taste

1. Set the air fryer to 200°C. Arrange the bacon strips in a single layer in the air fryer basket—some overlapping is okay because the bacon will shrink, but cook in batches if needed. Air fry for 8 minutes. Flip the bacon strips and air fry for 2 to 5 minutes more, until the bacon is crisp. Remove the bacon from the air fryer. 2. Put the tomatoes in the air fryer basket and air fry for 3 to 5 minutes, until they are just starting to burst. Remove the tomatoes from the air fryer. 3. Put the courgette noodles in the air fryer and air fry for 2 to 4 minutes, to the desired doneness. 4. Meanwhile, combine the ricotta, cream, and Parmesan in a saucepan over medium-low heat. Cook, stirring often, until warm and combined. 5. Crumble the bacon. Place the courgette, bacon, and tomatoes in a bowl. Toss with the ricotta sauce. Season with salt and pepper, and sprinkle with additional Parmesan.

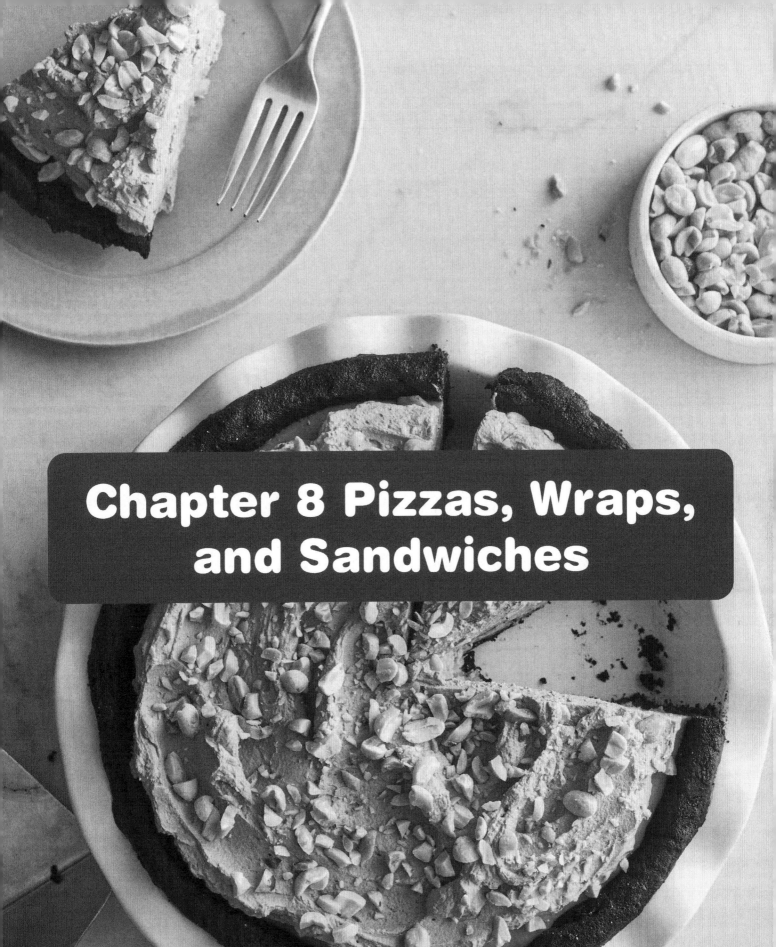

Chapter 8 Pizzas, Wraps, and Sandwiches

Chapter 8 Pizzas, Wraps, and Sandwiches

Cheesy Veggie Wraps

Prep time: 15 minutes | Cook time: 8 to 10 minutes per batch | Serves 4

227 g green beans
2 portobello mushroom caps, sliced
1 large red pepper, sliced
2 tablespoons olive oil, divided
¼ teaspoon salt
1 (425 g) can chickpeas, drained
3 tablespoons lemon juice
¼ teaspoon ground black pepper
4 (6-inch) wholemeal wraps
110 g fresh herb or garlic goat cheese, crumbled
1 lemon, cut into wedges

Preheat the air fryer to 200ºC. Add the green beans, mushrooms, red pepper to a large bowl. Drizzle with 1 tablespoon olive oil and season with salt. Toss until well coated. Transfer the vegetable mixture to a baking pan. Air fry in the preheated air fryer in 2 batches, 8 to 10 minutes per batch, stirring constantly during cooking. Meanwhile, mash the chickpeas with lemon juice, pepper and the remaining 1 tablespoon oil until well blended Unfold the wraps on a clean work surface. Spoon the chickpea mash on the wraps and spread all over. Divide the cooked veggies among wraps. Sprinkle 30 g crumbled goat cheese on top of each wrap. Fold to wrap. Squeeze the lemon wedges on top and serve.

Cabbage and Mushroom Spring Rolls

Prep time: 20 minutes | Cook time: 35 minutes | Makes 14 spring rolls

2 tablespoons vegetable oil
1 L sliced Chinese leaf
142 g shiitake mushrooms, diced
3 carrots, cut into thin matchsticks
1 tablespoon minced fresh ginger
1 tablespoon minced garlic
1 bunch spring onions, white
and light green parts only, sliced
2 tablespoons soy sauce
1 (113 g) package cellophane noodles or vermicelli
¼ teaspoon cornflour
1 (340 g) package frozen spring roll wrappers, thawed
Cooking spray

Heat the olive oil in a non-stick skillet over medium-high heat until shimmering. Add the Chinese leaf, mushrooms, and carrots and sauté for 3 minutes or until tender. Add the ginger, garlic, and spring onions and sauté for 1 minutes or until fragrant. Mix in the soy sauce and turn off the heat. Discard any liquid remains in the skillet and allow to cool for a few minutes. Bring a pot of water to a boil, then turn off the heat and pour in the noodles. Let sit for 10 minutes or until the noodles are al dente. Transfer 235 ml of the noodles in the skillet and toss with the cooked vegetables. Reserve the remaining noodles for other use. Dissolve the cornflour in a small dish of water, then place the wrappers on a clean work surface. Dab the edges of the wrappers with cornflour. Scoop up 3 tablespoons of filling in the centre of each wrapper, then fold the corner in front of you over the filling. Tuck the wrapper under the filling, then fold the corners on both sides into the centre. Keep rolling to seal the wrapper. Repeat with remaining wrappers. Preheat the air fryer to 200ºC and spritz with cooking spray. Arrange the wrappers in the preheated air fryer and spritz with cooking spray. Air fry in batches for 10 minutes or until golden brown. Flip the wrappers halfway through. Serve immediately.

Crunchy Chicken and Ranch Wraps

Prep time: 10 minutes | Cook time: 25 minutes | Serves 4

2 (113 g) boneless, skinless breasts
30 ml ranch dressing
Chicken seasoning or rub
235 ml plain flour
1 egg
120 ml breadcrumbs
Cooking oil
4 medium (8-inch) flour tortillas
350 ml shredded lettuce
3 tablespoons ranch dressing

With your knife blade parallel to the cutting board, slice the chicken breasts in half horizontally to create 4 thin cutlets. Season the chicken cutlets with the ranch dressing and chicken seasoning to taste. In a bowl large enough to dip a chicken cutlet, beat the egg. In another bowl, place the flour. Put the breadcrumbs in a third bowl. Spray the air fryer basket with cooking oil. Dip each chicken cutlet in the flour, then the egg, and then the breadcrumbs. Place the chicken in the air fryer. Do not stack. Cook in batches. Spray the chicken with cooking oil. Air fry at 370ºF for 7 minutes. Open the air fryer and flip the chicken. Cook for an additional 3 to 4 minutes, until crisp. Remove the cooked chicken from the air fryer and allow to cool for 2 to 3 minutes. Repeat steps 6 through 8 for the remaining chicken. Cut the chicken into strips. Divide the chicken strips, shredded lettuce, and ranch dressing evenly among the tortillas and serve.

Pesto Chicken Mini Pizzas

Prep time: 5 minutes | Cook time: 10 minutes | Serves 4

475 ml shredded cooked chicken

180 ml pesto

4 English muffins, split

475 ml shredded Mozzarella cheese

In a medium bowl, toss the chicken with the pesto. Place one-eighth of the chicken on each English muffin half. Top each English muffin with 60 ml Mozzarella cheese. Put four pizzas at a time in the air fryer and air fry at 175ºC for 5 minutes. Repeat this process with the other four pizzas.

Beans and Greens Pizza

Prep time: 11 minutes | Cook time: 14 to 19 minutes | Serves 4

180 ml wholemeal pastry flour

½ teaspoon low-salt baking powder

1 tablespoon olive oil, divided

235 ml chopped kale

475 ml chopped fresh baby spinach

235 ml canned no-added-salt cannellini beans, rinsed and drained

½ teaspoon dried thyme

1 piece low-salt string cheese, torn into pieces

In a small bowl, mix the pastry flour and baking powder until well combined. Add 60 ml water and 2 teaspoons of olive oil. Mix until a dough forms. On a floured surface, press or roll the dough into a 7-inch round. Set aside while you cook the greens. In a baking pan, mix the kale, spinach, and remaining teaspoon of the olive oil. Air fry at 175ºC for 3 to 5 minutes, until the greens are wilted. Drain well. Put the pizza dough into the air fryer basket. Top with the greens, cannellini beans, thyme, and string cheese. Air fry for 11 to 14 minutes, or until the crust is golden brown and the cheese is melted. Cut into quarters to serve.

Cheesy Chicken Sandwich

Prep time: 10 minutes | Cook time: 5 to 7 minutes | Serves 1

80 ml chicken, cooked and shredded

2 Mozzarella slices

1 hamburger bun

60 ml shredded cabbage

1 teaspoon mayonnaise

2 teaspoons butter, melted

1 teaspoon olive oil

½ teaspoon balsamic vinegar

¼ teaspoon smoked paprika

¼ teaspoon black pepper

¼ teaspoon garlic powder

Pinch of salt

Preheat the air fryer to 190ºC. Brush some butter onto the outside of the hamburger bun. In a bowl, coat the chicken with the garlic powder, salt, pepper, and paprika. In a separate bowl, stir together the mayonnaise, olive oil, cabbage, and balsamic vinegar to make coleslaw. Slice the bun in two. Start building the sandwich, starting with the chicken, followed by the Mozzarella, the coleslaw, and finally the top bun. Transfer the sandwich to the air fryer and bake for 5 to 7 minutes. Serve immediately.

Bacon Garlic Pizza

Prep time: 10 minutes | Cook time: 20 minutes | Serves 4

Flour, for dusting

Non-stick baking spray with flour

4 frozen large wholemeal bread rolls, thawed

5 cloves garlic, minced

180 ml pizza sauce

½ teaspoon dried oregano

½ teaspoon garlic salt

8 slices precooked bacon, cut into 1-inch pieces

300 ml shredded Cheddar cheese

On a lightly floured surface, press out each bread roll to a 5-by-3-inch oval. Spray four 6-by-4-inch pieces of heavy-duty foil with non-stick spray and place one crust on each piece. Bake, two at a time, at 190ºC for 2 minutes or until the crusts are set, but not browned. Meanwhile, in a small bowl, combine the garlic, pizza sauce, oregano, and garlic salt. When the pizza crusts are set, spread each with some of the sauce. Top with the bacon pieces and Cheddar cheese. Bake, two at a time, for another 8 minutes or until the crust is browned and the cheese is melted and starting to brown.

Portobello Pizzas

Prep time: 10 minutes | Cook time: 10 minutes | Serves 4

Olive oil

4 large portobello mushroom caps, cleaned and stems removed

Garlic powder

8 tablespoons pizza sauce

16 slices turkey pepperoni

8 tablespoons Mozzarella cheese

Spray the air fryer basket lightly with olive oil. Lightly spray the outside of the mushrooms with olive oil and sprinkle with a little garlic powder, to taste. Turn the mushroom over and lightly spray the sides and top edges of the mushroom with olive oil and sprinkle with garlic powder, to taste. Place the mushrooms in the air fryer basket in a single layer with the top side down. Leave room between the mushrooms. You may need to cook them in batches. Air fry at 175ºC for 5 minutes. Spoon 2 tablespoons of pizza sauce on each mushroom. Top each with 4 slices of turkey pepperoni and sprinkle with 2 tablespoons of Mozzarella cheese. Press the pepperoni and cheese down into the pizza sauce to help prevent it from flying around inside the air fryer. Air fry until the cheese is melted and lightly browned on top, another 3 to 5 minutes.

Beef and Pepper Fajitas

Prep time: 15 minutes | Cook time: 10 minutes | Serves 4

450 g beef sirloin steak, cut into strips	1 tablespoon paprika
2 shallots, sliced	Salt and ground black pepper, to taste
1 orange pepper, sliced	4 corn tortillas
1 red pepper, sliced	120 ml shredded Cheddar cheese
2 garlic cloves, minced	
2 tablespoons Cajun seasoning	Cooking spray

Preheat the air fryer to 180°C and spritz with cooking spray. Combine all the ingredients, except for the tortillas and cheese, in a large bowl. Toss to coat well. Pour the beef and vegetables in the preheated air fryer and spritz with cooking spray. Air fry for 10 minutes or until the meat is browned and the vegetables are soft and lightly wilted. Shake the basket halfway through. Unfold the tortillas on a clean work surface and spread the cooked beef and vegetables on top. Scatter with cheese and fold to serve.

Grilled Cheese Sandwich

Prep time: 5 minutes | Cook time: 5 minutes | Makes 2 sandwiches

4 slices bread	2 teaspoons butter or oil
110 g Cheddar cheese slices	

Lay the four cheese slices on two of the bread slices and top with the remaining two slices of bread. Brush both sides with butter or oil and cut the sandwiches in rectangular halves. Place in air fryer basket and air fry at 200°C for 5 minutes until the outside is crisp and the cheese melts.

Turkey-Hummus Wraps

Prep time: 10 minutes | Cook time: 3 to 7 minutes per batch | Serves 4

4 large wholemeal wraps	8 slices provolone cheese
120 ml hummus	235 ml fresh baby spinach (or more to taste)
16 thin slices deli turkey	

To assemble, place 2 tablespoons of hummus on each wrap and spread to within about a half inch from edges. Top with 4 slices of turkey and 2 slices of provolone. Finish with 60 ml baby spinach or pile on as much as you like. Roll up each wrap. You don't need to fold or seal the ends. Place 2 wraps in air fryer basket, seam side down. Air fry at 180°C for 3 to 4 minutes to warm filling and melt cheese. If you like, you can continue cooking for 2 or 3 more minutes, until the wrap is slightly crispy. Repeat step 4 to cook remaining wraps.

Shrimp and Courgette Curry Potstickers

Prep time: 35 minutes | Cook time: 15 minutes | Serves 10

230 g peeled and deveined shrimp, finely chopped	1 tablespoon green curry paste
1 medium courgette, coarsely grated	2 spring onions, thinly sliced
	60 ml basil, chopped
1 tablespoon fish sauce	30 round dumpling wrappers
	Cooking spray

Combine the chopped shrimp, courgette, fish sauce, curry paste, spring onions, and basil in a large bowl. Stir to mix well. Unfold the dumpling wrappers on a clean work surface, dab a little water around the edges of each wrapper, then scoop up 1 teaspoon of filling in the middle of each wrapper. Make the potstickers: Fold the wrappers in half and press the edges to seal. Preheat the air fryer to 175°C. Spritz the air fryer basket with cooking spray. Transfer 10 potstickers in the basket each time and spritz with cooking spray. Air fry for 5 minutes or until the potstickers are crunchy and lightly browned. Flip the potstickers halfway through. Repeat with remaining potstickers. Serve immediately.

Avocado and Slaw Tacos

Prep time: 15 minutes | Cook time: 6 minutes | Serves 4

60 ml plain flour	sliced
¼ teaspoon salt, plus more as needed	1 deseeded jalapeño, thinly sliced
¼ teaspoon ground black pepper	2 spring onions, thinly sliced
2 large egg whites	120 ml coriander leaves
300 ml panko breadcrumbs	60 ml mayonnaise
2 tablespoons olive oil	Juice and zest of 1 lime
2 avocados, peeled and halved, cut into ½-inch-thick slices	4 corn tortillas, warmed
	120 ml sour cream
½ small red cabbage, thinly	Cooking spray

Preheat the air fryer to 200°C. Spritz the air fryer basket with cooking spray. Pour the flour in a large bowl and sprinkle with salt and black pepper, then stir to mix well. Whisk the egg whites in a separate bowl. Combine the panko with olive oil on a shallow dish. Dredge the avocado slices in the bowl of flour, then into the egg to coat. Shake the excess off, then roll the slices over the panko. Arrange the avocado slices in a single layer in the basket and spritz the cooking spray. Air fry for 6 minutes or until tender and lightly browned. Flip the slices halfway through with tongs. Combine the cabbage, jalapeño, onions, coriander leaves, mayo, lime juice and zest, and a touch of salt in a separate large bowl. Toss to mix well. Unfold the tortillas on a clean work surface, then spread with cabbage slaw and air fried avocados. Top with sour cream and serve.

Chicken and Pickles Sandwich

Prep time: 30 minutes | Cook time: 25 minutes | Serves 4

2 (113 g) boneless, skinless chicken breasts	1 egg
235 ml dill pickle juice	120 ml plain flour
235 ml milk, divided	Salt and pepper, to taste
Cooking oil	4 buns
	Pickles

With your knife blade parallel to the cutting board, slice the chicken breasts in half horizontally to create 4 thin cutlets. Place the chicken in a large bowl. Add the pickle juice and 120 ml of milk and toss to coat. Allow the chicken to marinate in the refrigerator for at least 30 minutes. Spray the air fryer basket with cooking oil. In a bowl large enough to dip a chicken cutlet, beat the egg and add the remaining 120 ml of milk. Stir to combine. In another bowl, place the flour and season with salt and pepper. When done marinating, dip each chicken cutlet in the egg and milk mixture and then the flour. Place 2 chicken cutlets in the air fryer. Spray them with cooking oil. Air fry at 370°F for 6 minutes. Open the air fryer and flip the chicken. Cook for an additional 6 minutes. Remove the cooked chicken from the air fryer, then repeat steps 7 and 8 for the remaining 2 chicken cutlets. Serve on buns with pickles.

Pea and Potato Samosas with Chutney

Prep time: 30 minutes | Cook time: 1 hour 10 minutes | Makes 16 samosas

Dough:	120 ml peas, thawed if frozen
1 L plain flour, plus more for flouring the work surface	475 ml mashed potatoes
	2 tablespoons yoghurt
60 ml plain yoghurt	Cooking spray
120 ml cold unsalted butter, cut into cubes	Chutney:
	235 ml mint leaves, lightly packed
2 teaspoons rock salt	
235 ml melted ice	475 ml coriander leaves, lightly packed
Filling:	
2 tablespoons vegetable oil	1 green chilli pepper, deseeded and minced
1 onion, diced	
1½ teaspoons coriander	120 ml minced onion
1½ teaspoons cumin	Juice of 1 lime
1 clove garlic, minced	1 teaspoon granulated sugar
1 teaspoon turmeric	1 teaspoon rock salt
1 teaspoon rock salt	2 tablespoons vegetable oil

Put the flour, yoghurt, butter, and salt in a food processor. Pulse to combine until grainy. Pour in the water and pulse until a smooth and firm dough forms. Transfer the dough on a clean and lightly floured working surface. Knead the dough and shape it into a ball. Cut in half and flatten the halves into 2 discs. Wrap them in plastic and let sit in refrigerator until ready to use. Meanwhile, make the filling: Heat the vegetable oil in a saucepan over medium heat. Add the onion and sauté for 5 minutes or until lightly browned. Add the coriander, cumin, garlic, turmeric, and salt and sauté for 2 minutes or until fragrant. Add the peas, potatoes, and yoghurt and stir to combine well. Turn off the heat and allow to cool. Meanwhile, combine the ingredients for the chutney in a food processor. Pulse to mix well until glossy. Pour the chutney in a bowl and refrigerate until ready to use. Make the samosas: Remove the dough discs from the refrigerator and cut each disc into 8 parts. Shape each part into a ball, then roll the ball into a 6-inch circle. Cut the circle in half and roll each half into a cone. Scoop up 2 tablespoons of the filling into the cone, press the edges of the cone to seal and form into a triangle. Repeat with remaining dough and filling. Preheat the air fryer to 180°C and spritz with cooking spray. Arrange four samosas each batch in the preheated air fryer and spritz with cooking spray. Air fry for 15 minutes or until golden brown and crispy. Flip the samosas halfway through. Serve the samosas with the chutney.

Bacon and Pepper Sandwiches

Prep time: 15 minutes | Cook time: 7 minutes | Serves 4

80 ml spicy barbecue sauce	1 yellow pepper, sliced
2 tablespoons honey	3 pitta pockets, cut in half
8 slices precooked bacon, cut into thirds	300 ml torn butterhead lettuce leaves
1 red pepper, sliced	2 tomatoes, sliced

In a small bowl, combine the barbecue sauce and the honey. Brush this mixture lightly onto the bacon slices and the red and yellow pepper slices. Put the peppers into the air fryer basket and air fry at 175°C for 4 minutes. Then shake the basket, add the bacon, and air fry for 2 minutes or until the bacon is browned and the peppers are tender. Fill the pitta halves with the bacon, peppers, any remaining barbecue sauce, lettuce, and tomatoes, and serve immediately.

Mushroom Pitta Pizzas

Prep time: 10 minutes | Cook time: 5 minutes | Serves 4

4 (3-inch) pittas	½ teaspoon dried basil
1 tablespoon olive oil	2 spring onions, minced
180 ml pizza sauce	235 ml grated Mozzarella or provolone cheese
1 (113 g) jar sliced mushrooms, drained	
	235 ml sliced grape tomatoes

Brush each piece of pitta with oil and top with the pizza sauce. Add the mushrooms and sprinkle with basil and spring onions. Top with the grated cheese. Bake at 180°C for 3 to 6 minutes or until cheese is melted and starts to brown. Top with the grape tomatoes and serve immediately.

Jerk Chicken Wraps

Prep time: 30 minutes | Cook time: 15 minutes | Serves 4

450 g boneless, skinless chicken tenderloins

235 ml jerk marinade

Olive oil

4 large low-carb tortillas

235 ml julienned carrots

235 ml peeled cucumber ribbons

235 ml shredded lettuce

235 ml mango or pineapple chunks

In a medium bowl, coat the chicken with the jerk marinade, cover, and refrigerate for 1 hour. Spray the air fryer basket lightly with olive oil. Place the chicken in the air fryer basket in a single layer and spray lightly with olive oil. You may need to cook the chicken in batches. Reserve any leftover marinade. Air fry at 190ºC for 8 minutes. Turn the chicken over and brush with some of the remaining marinade. Cook until the chicken reaches an internal temperature of at least 75ºC, an additional 5 to 7 minutes. To assemble the wraps, fill each tortilla with 60 ml carrots, 60 ml cucumber, 60 ml lettuce, and 60 ml mango. Place one quarter of the chicken tenderloins on top and roll up the tortilla. These are great served warm or cold.

Spinach and Ricotta Pockets

Prep time: 20 minutes | Cook time: 10 minutes per batch | Makes 8 pockets

2 large eggs, divided

1 tablespoon water

235 ml baby spinach, roughly chopped

60 ml sun-dried tomatoes, finely chopped

235 ml ricotta cheese

235 ml basil, chopped

¼ teaspoon red pepper flakes

¼ teaspoon rock salt

2 refrigerated rolled sheets of shortcrust pastry

2 tablespoons sesame seeds

Preheat the air fryer to 190ºC. Spritz the air fryer basket with cooking spray. Whisk an egg with water in a small bowl. Combine the spinach, tomatoes, the other egg, ricotta cheese, basil, red pepper flakes, and salt in a large bowl. Whisk to mix well. Unfold the pastry on a clean work surface and slice each sheet into 4 wedges. Scoop up 3 tablespoons of the spinach mixture on each wedge and leave ½ inch space from edges. Fold the wedges in half to wrap the filling and press the edges with a fork to seal. Arrange the wraps in the preheated air fryer and spritz with cooking spray. Sprinkle with sesame seeds. Work in 4 batches to avoid overcrowding. Air fry for 10 minutes or until crispy and golden. Flip them halfway through. Serve immediately.

Turkish Pizza

Prep time: 20 minutes | Cook time: 10 minutes | Serves 4

110 g minced lamb or 15% fat minced beef

60 ml finely chopped green pepper

60 ml chopped fresh parsley

1 small plum tomato, seeded and finely chopped

2 tablespoons finely chopped brown onion

1 garlic clove, minced

2 teaspoons tomato paste

¼ teaspoon sweet paprika

¼ teaspoon ground cumin

⅛ to ¼ teaspoon red pepper flakes

⅛ teaspoon ground allspice

⅛ teaspoon rock salt

⅛ teaspoon black pepper

4 (6-inch) flour tortillas

For Serving:

Chopped fresh mint

Extra-virgin olive oil

Lemon wedges

In a medium bowl, gently mix the lamb, pepper, parsley, chopped tomato, onion, garlic, tomato paste, paprika, cumin, red pepper flakes, allspice, salt, and black pepper until well combined. Divide the meat mixture evenly among the tortillas, spreading it all the way to the edge of each tortilla. Place 1 tortilla in the air fryer basket. Set the air fryer to 200ºC for 10 minutes, or until the meat topping has browned and the edge of the tortilla is golden. Transfer to a plate and repeat to cook the remaining tortillas. Serve the pizzas warm, topped with chopped fresh mint and a drizzle of extra-virgin olive oil and with lemon wedges alongside.

Chapter 9 Vegetables and Sides

Chapter 9 Vegetables and Sides

Stuffed Red Peppers with Herbed Ricotta and Tomatoes

Prep time: 10 minutes | Cook time: 20 minutes | Serves 4

2 red peppers
250 g cooked brown rice
2 plum tomatoes, diced
1 garlic clove, minced
¼ teaspoon salt
¼ teaspoon black pepper
115 g ricotta

3 tablespoons fresh basil, chopped
3 tablespoons fresh oregano, chopped
20 g shredded Parmesan, for topping

1. Preheat the air fryer to 180ºC. 2. Cut the bell peppers in half and remove the seeds and stem. 3. In a medium bowl, combine the brown rice, tomatoes, garlic, salt, and pepper. 4. Distribute the rice filling evenly among the four bell pepper halves. 5. In a small bowl, combine the ricotta, basil, and oregano. Put the herbed cheese over the top of the rice mixture in each bell pepper. 6. Place the bell peppers into the air fryer and roast for 20 minutes. 7. Remove and serve with shredded Parmesan on top.

Super Cheesy Gold Aubergine

Prep time: 15 minutes | Cook time: 30 minutes | Serves 4

1 medium aubergine, peeled and cut into ½-inch-thick rounds
1 teaspoon salt, plus more for seasoning
60 g plain flour
2 eggs
90 g Italian bread crumbs
2 tablespoons grated Parmesan

cheese
Freshly ground black pepper, to taste
Cooking oil spray
180 g marinara sauce
45 g shredded Parmesan cheese, divided
110 g shredded Mozzarella cheese, divided

1. Blot the aubergine with paper towels to dry completely. You can also sprinkle with 1 teaspoon of salt to sweat out the moisture; if you do this, rinse the aubergine slices and blot dry again. 2. Place the flour in a shallow bowl. 3. In another shallow bowl, beat the eggs. 4. In a third shallow bowl, stir together the bread crumbs and grated Parmesan cheese and season with salt and pepper. 5. Dip each aubergine round in the flour, in the eggs, and into the bread crumbs to coat. 6. Insert the crisper plate into the basket and the basket into the unit. Preheat the unit by selecting AIR FRY, setting the temperature to 200ºC, and setting the time to 3 minutes. Select

START/STOP to begin. 7. Once the unit is preheated, spray the crisper plate and the basket with cooking oil. Working in batches, place the aubergine rounds into the basket. Do not stack them. Spray the aubergine with the cooking oil. 8. Select AIR FRY, set the temperature to 200ºC, and set the time to 10 minutes. Select START/STOP to begin. 9. After 7 minutes, open the unit and top each round with 1 teaspoon of marinara sauce and ½ tablespoon each of shredded Parmesan and Mozzarella cheese. Resume cooking for 2 to 3 minutes until the cheese melts. 10. Repeat steps 5, 6, 7, 8, and 9 with the remaining aubergine. 11. When the cooking is complete, serve immediately.

Buttery Green Beans

Prep time: 5 minutes | Cook time: 8 to 10 minutes | Serves 6

450 g green beans, trimmed
1 tablespoon avocado oil
1 teaspoon garlic powder
Sea salt and freshly ground black pepper, to taste

4 tablespoons unsalted butter, melted
20 g freshly grated Parmesan cheese

1. In a large bowl, toss together the green beans, avocado oil, and garlic powder and season with salt and pepper. 2. Set the air fryer to 200ºC. Arrange the green beans in a single layer in the air fryer basket. Air fry for 8 to 10 minutes, tossing halfway through. 3. Transfer the beans to a large bowl and toss with the melted butter. Top with the Parmesan cheese and serve warm.

Burger Bun for One

Prep time: 2 minutes | Cook time: 5 minutes | Serves 1

2 tablespoons salted butter, melted
25 g blanched finely ground almond flour

¼ teaspoon baking powder
⅛ teaspoon apple cider vinegar
1 large egg, whisked

1. Pour butter into an ungreased ramekin. Add flour, baking powder, and vinegar to ramekin and stir until combined. Add egg and stir until batter is mostly smooth. 2. Place ramekin into air fryer basket. Adjust the temperature to 180ºC and bake for 5 minutes. When done, the centre will be firm and the top slightly browned. Let cool, about 5 minutes, then remove from ramekin and slice in half. Serve.

Rosemary-Roasted Red Potatoes

Prep time: 5 minutes | Cook time: 20 minutes | Serves 6

450 g red potatoes, quartered	¼ teaspoon black pepper
65 ml olive oil	1 garlic clove, minced
½ teaspoon coarse sea salt	4 rosemary sprigs

1. Preheat the air fryer to 180ºC. 2. In a large bowl, toss the potatoes with the olive oil, salt, pepper, and garlic until well coated. 3. Pour the potatoes into the air fryer basket and top with the sprigs of rosemary. 4. Roast for 10 minutes, then stir or toss the potatoes and roast for 10 minutes more. 5. Remove the rosemary sprigs and serve the potatoes. Season with additional salt and pepper, if needed.

Tahini-Lemon Kale

Prep time: 5 minutes | Cook time: 15 minutes | Serves 2 to 4

60 g tahini	110 g packed torn kale leaves
60 ml fresh lemon juice	(stems and ribs removed and
2 tablespoons olive oil	leaves torn into palm-size
1 teaspoon sesame seeds	pieces)
½ teaspoon garlic powder	coarse sea salt and freshly
¼ teaspoon cayenne pepper	ground black pepper, to taste

1. In a large bowl, whisk together the tahini, lemon juice, olive oil, sesame seeds, garlic powder, and cayenne until smooth. Add the kale leaves, season with salt and black pepper, and toss in the dressing until completely coated. Transfer the kale leaves to a cake pan. 2. Place the pan in the air fryer and roast at 180ºC, stirring every 5 minutes, until the kale is wilted and the top is lightly browned, about 15 minutes. Remove the pan from the air fryer and serve warm.

Bacon Potatoes and Green Beans

Prep time: 10 minutes | Cook time: 25 minutes | Serves 4

Oil, for spraying	280 g fresh green beans
900 g medium Maris Piper potatoes, quartered	1 teaspoon salt
100 g bacon bits	½ teaspoon freshly ground black pepper

1. Line the air fryer basket with parchment and spray lightly with oil. 2. Place the potatoes in the prepared basket. Top with the bacon bits and green beans. Sprinkle with the salt and black pepper and spray liberally with oil. 3. Air fry at 180ºC for 25 minutes, stirring after 12 minutes and spraying with oil, until the potatoes are easily pierced with a fork.

Tofu Bites

Prep time: 15 minutes | Cook time: 30 minutes | Serves 4

1 packaged firm tofu, cubed and pressed to remove excess water	1 teaspoon hot sauce
1 tablespoon soy sauce	2 tablespoons sesame seeds
1 tablespoon ketchup	1 teaspoon garlic powder
1 tablespoon maple syrup	Salt and ground black pepper, to taste
½ teaspoon vinegar	Cooking spray
1 teaspoon liquid smoke	

1. Preheat the air fryer to 190ºC. 2. Spritz a baking dish with cooking spray. 3. Combine all the ingredients to coat the tofu completely and allow the marinade to absorb for half an hour. 4. Transfer the tofu to the baking dish, then air fry for 15 minutes. Flip the tofu over and air fry for another 15 minutes on the other side. 5. Serve immediately.

Potato with Creamy Cheese

Prep time: 5 minutes | Cook time: 15 minutes | Serves 2

2 medium potatoes	1 teaspoon chives
1 teaspoon butter	1½ tablespoons grated
3 tablespoons sour cream	Parmesan cheese

1. Preheat the air fryer to 180ºC. 2. Pierce the potatoes with a fork and boil them in water until they are cooked. 3. Transfer to the air fryer and air fry for 15 minutes. 4. In the meantime, combine the sour cream, cheese and chives in a bowl. Cut the potatoes halfway to open them up and fill with the butter and sour cream mixture. 5. Serve immediately.

Blistered Shishito Peppers with Lime Juice

Prep time: 5 minutes | Cook time: 9 minutes | Serves 3

230 g shishito peppers, rinsed	1 tablespoon tamari or shoyu
Cooking spray	2 teaspoons fresh lime juice
Sauce:	2 large garlic cloves, minced

1. Preheat the air fryer to 200ºC. Spritz the air fryer basket with cooking spray. 2. Place the shishito peppers in the basket and spritz them with cooking spray. Roast for 3 minutes. 3. Meanwhile, whisk together all the ingredients for the sauce in a large bowl. Set aside. 4. Shake the basket and spritz them with cooking spray again, then roast for an additional 3 minutes. 5. Shake the basket one more time and spray the peppers with cooking spray. Continue roasting for 3 minutes until the peppers are blistered and nicely browned. 6. Remove the peppers from the basket to the bowl of sauce. Toss to coat well and serve immediately.

Curry Roasted Cauliflower

Prep time: 10 minutes | Cook time: 20 minutes | Serves 4

65 ml olive oil	1 head cauliflower, cut into
2 teaspoons curry powder	bite-size florets
½ teaspoon salt	½ red onion, sliced
¼ teaspoon freshly ground	2 tablespoons freshly chopped
black pepper	parsley, for garnish (optional)

1. Preheat the air fryer to 200ºC. 2. In a large bowl, combine the olive oil, curry powder, salt, and pepper. Add the cauliflower and onion. Toss gently until the vegetables are completely coated with the oil mixture. Transfer the vegetables to the basket of the air fryer. 3. Pausing about halfway through the cooking time to shake the basket, air fry for 20 minutes until the cauliflower is tender and beginning to brown. Top with the parsley, if desired, before serving.

Sweet and Crispy Roasted Pearl Onions

Prep time: 5 minutes | Cook time: 18 minutes | Serves 3

1 (410 g) package frozen pearl	2 teaspoons finely chopped
onions (do not thaw)	fresh rosemary
2 tablespoons extra-virgin olive	½ teaspoon coarse sea salt
oil	¼ teaspoon black pepper
2 tablespoons balsamic vinegar	

1. In a medium bowl, combine the onions, olive oil, vinegar, rosemary, salt, and pepper until well coated. 2. Transfer the onions to the air fryer basket. Set the air fryer to 200ºC for 18 minutes, or until the onions are tender and lightly charred, stirring once or twice during the cooking time.

Buffalo Cauliflower with Blue Cheese

Prep time: 15 minutes | Cook time: 5 to 7 minutes per batch | Serves 6

1 large head cauliflower, rinsed	190 g nonfat Greek yogurt
and separated into small florets	60 g buttermilk
1 tablespoon extra-virgin olive	½ teaspoon hot sauce
oil	1 celery stalk, chopped
½ teaspoon garlic powder	2 tablespoons crumbled blue
Cooking oil spray	cheese
80 ml hot wing sauce	

1. Insert the crisper plate into the basket and the basket into the unit. Preheat the unit by selecting AIR FRY, setting the temperature to190ºC, and setting the time to 3 minutes. Select START/STOP to begin. 2. In a large bowl, toss together the cauliflower florets and olive oil. Sprinkle with the garlic powder and toss again to coat. 3. Once the unit is preheated, spray the crisper plate with cooking oil.

Put half the cauliflower into the basket. 4. Select AIR FRY, set the temperature to190ºC, and set the time to 7 minutes. Select START/STOP to begin. 5. After 3 minutes, remove the basket and shake the cauliflower. Reinsert the basket to resume cooking. After 2 minutes, check the cauliflower. It is done when it is browned. If not, resume cooking. 6. When the cooking is complete, transfer the cauliflower to a serving bowl and toss with half the hot wing sauce. 7. Repeat steps 4, 5, and 6 with the remaining cauliflower and hot wing sauce. 8. In a small bowl, stir together the yogurt, buttermilk, hot sauce, celery, and blue cheese. Drizzle the sauce over the finished cauliflower and serve.

Spiced Honey-Walnut Carrots

Prep time: 5 minutes | Cook time: 12 minutes | Serves 6

450 g baby carrots	¼ teaspoon ground cinnamon
2 tablespoons olive oil	25 g black walnuts, chopped
80 g raw honey	

1. Preheat the air fryer to 180ºC. 2. In a large bowl, toss the baby carrots with olive oil, honey, and cinnamon until well coated. 3. Pour into the air fryer and roast for 6 minutes. Shake the basket, sprinkle the walnuts on top, and roast for 6 minutes more. 4. Remove the carrots from the air fryer and serve.

Broccoli-Cheddar Twice-Baked Potatoes

Prep time: 10 minutes | Cook time: 46 minutes | Serves 4

Oil, for spraying	1 tablespoon sour cream
2 medium Maris Piper potatoes	1 teaspoon garlic powder
1 tablespoon olive oil	1 teaspoon onion powder
30 g broccoli florets	60 g shredded Cheddar cheese

1. Line the air fryer basket with parchment and spray lightly with oil. 2. Rinse the potatoes and pat dry with paper towels. Rub the outside of the potatoes with the olive oil and place them in the prepared basket. 3. Air fry at 200ºC for 40 minutes, or until easily pierced with a fork. Let cool just enough to handle, then cut the potatoes in half lengthwise. 4. Meanwhile, place the broccoli in a microwave-safe bowl, cover with water, and microwave on high for 5 to 8 minutes. Drain and set aside. 5. Scoop out most of the potato flesh and transfer to a medium bowl. 6. Add the sour cream, garlic, and onion powder and stir until the potatoes are mashed. 7. Spoon the potato mixture back into the hollowed potato skins, mounding it to fit, if necessary. Top with the broccoli and cheese. Return the potatoes to the basket. You may need to work in batches, depending on the size of your air fryer. 8. Air fry at 200ºC for 3 to 6 minutes, or until the cheese has melted. Serve immediately.

Roasted Salsa

Prep time: 15 minutes | Cook time: 30 minutes | Makes 500 g

2 large San Marzano tomatoes, cored and cut into large chunks
½ medium white onion, peeled and large-diced
½ medium jalapeño, seeded and large-diced

2 cloves garlic, peeled and diced
½ teaspoon salt
1 tablespoon coconut oil
65 ml fresh lime juice

1. Place tomatoes, onion, and jalapeño into an ungreased round nonstick baking dish. Add garlic, then sprinkle with salt and drizzle with coconut oil. 2. Place dish into air fryer basket. Adjust the temperature to 150°C and bake for 30 minutes. Vegetables will be dark brown around the edges and tender when done. 3. Pour mixture into a food processor or blender. Add lime juice. Process on low speed 30 seconds until only a few chunks remain. 4. Transfer salsa to a sealable container and refrigerate at least 1 hour. Serve chilled.

Lemony Broccoli

Prep time: 10 minutes | Cook time: 9 to 14 minutes per batch | Serves 4

1 large head broccoli, rinsed and patted dry
2 teaspoons extra-virgin olive oil

1 tablespoon freshly squeezed lemon juice
Olive oil spray

1. Cut off the broccoli florets and separate them. You can use the stems, too; peel the stems and cut them into 1-inch chunks. 2. Insert the crisper plate into the basket and the basket into the unit. Preheat the unit by selecting AIR ROAST, setting the temperature to 200°C, and setting the time to 3 minutes. Select START/STOP to begin. 3. In a large bowl, toss together the broccoli, olive oil, and lemon juice until coated. 4. Once the unit is preheated, spray the crisper plate with olive oil. Working in batches, place half the broccoli into the basket. 5. Select AIR ROAST, set the temperature to 200°C, and set the time to 14 minutes. Select START/STOP to begin. 6. After 5 minutes, remove the basket and shake the broccoli. Reinsert the basket to resume cooking. Check the broccoli after 5 minutes. If it is crisp-tender and slightly brown around the edges, it is done. If not, resume cooking. 7. When the cooking is complete, transfer the broccoli to a serving bowl. Repeat steps 5 and 6 with the remaining broccoli. Serve immediately.

Green Peas with Mint

Prep time: 5 minutes | Cook time: 5 minutes | Serves 4

75 g shredded lettuce
1 (280 g) package frozen green peas, thawed

1 tablespoon fresh mint, shredded
1 teaspoon melted butter

1. Lay the shredded lettuce in the air fryer basket. 2. Toss together the peas, mint, and melted butter and spoon over the lettuce. 3. Air fry at 180°C for 5 minutes, until peas are warm and lettuce wilts.

Zesty Fried Asparagus

Prep time: 3 minutes | Cook time: 10 minutes | Serves 4

Oil, for spraying
10 to 12 spears asparagus, trimmed
2 tablespoons olive oil

1 tablespoon garlic powder
1 teaspoon chili powder
½ teaspoon ground cumin
¼ teaspoon salt

1. Line the air fryer basket with parchment and spray lightly with oil. 2. If the asparagus are too long to fit easily in the air fryer, cut them in half. 3. Place the asparagus, olive oil, garlic, chili powder, cumin, and salt in a zip-top plastic bag, seal, and toss until evenly coated. 4. Place the asparagus in the prepared basket. 5. Roast at 200°C for 5 minutes, flip, and cook for another 5 minutes, or until bright green and firm but tender.

Spiced Butternut Squash

Prep time: 10 minutes | Cook time: 15 minutes | Serves 4

600 g 1-inch-cubed butternut squash
2 tablespoons vegetable oil

1 to 2 tablespoons brown sugar
1 teaspoon Chinese five-spice powder

1. In a medium bowl, combine the squash, oil, sugar, and five-spice powder. Toss to coat. 2. Place the squash in the air fryer basket. Set the air fryer to 200°C for 15 minutes or until tender.

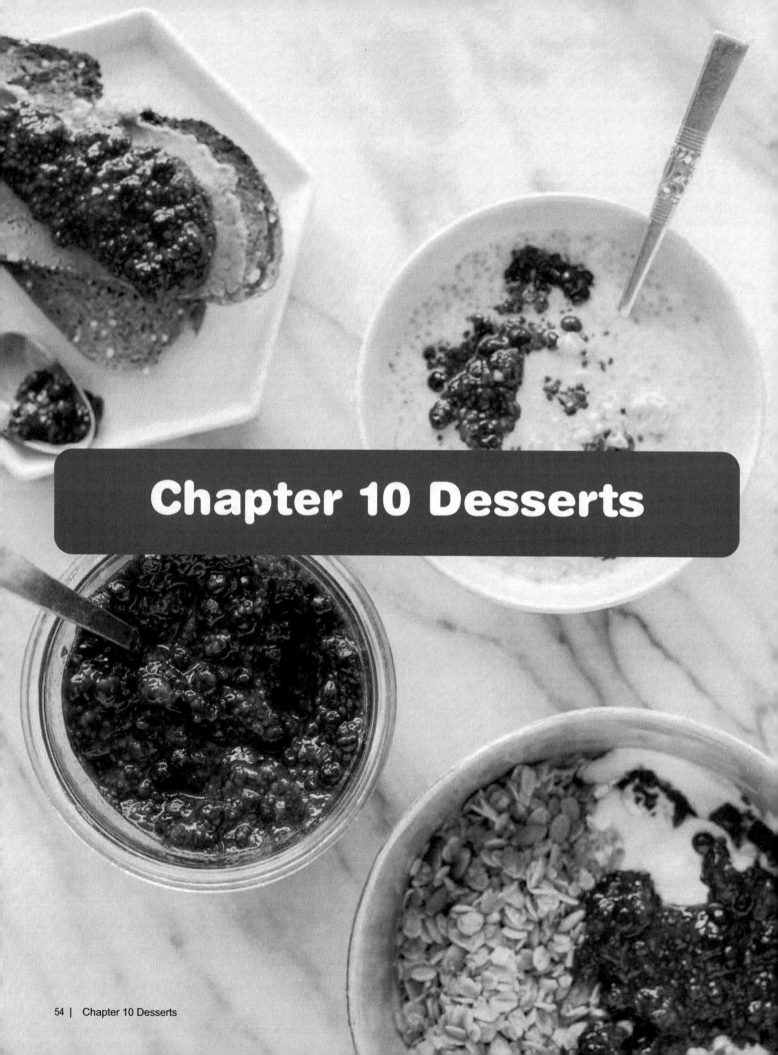

Chapter 10 Desserts

Chapter 10 Desserts

Simple Pineapple Sticks

Prep time: 5 minutes | Cook time: 10 minutes | Serves 4

½ fresh pineapple, cut into sticks

25 g desiccated coconut

1. Preheat the air fryer to 200ºC. 2. Coat the pineapple sticks in the desiccated coconut and put each one in the air fryer basket. 3. Air fry for 10 minutes. 4. Serve immediately

Coconut-Custard Pie

Prep time: 10 minutes | Cook time: 20 to 23 minutes | Serves 4

240 ml milk

50 g granulated sugar, plus 2 tablespoons

30 g scone mix

1 teaspoon vanilla extract

2 eggs

2 tablespoons melted butter

Cooking spray

50 g desiccated, sweetened coconut

1. Place all ingredients except coconut in a medium bowl. 2. Using a hand mixer, beat on high speed for 3 minutes. 3. Let sit for 5 minutes. 4. Preheat the air fryer to 165ºC. 5. Spray a baking pan with cooking spray and place pan in air fryer basket. 6. Pour filling into pan and sprinkle coconut over top. 7. Cook pie for 20 to 23 minutes or until center sets.

Chickpea Brownies

Prep time: 10 minutes | Cook time: 20 minutes | Serves 6

Vegetable oil

425 g can chickpeas, drained and rinsed

4 large eggs

80 ml coconut oil, melted

80 ml honey

3 tablespoons unsweetened

cocoa powder

1 tablespoon espresso powder (optional)

1 teaspoon baking powder

1 teaspoon baking soda

80 g chocolate chips

1. Preheat the air fryer to 165ºC. 2. Generously grease a baking pan with vegetable oil. 3. In a blender or food processor, combine the chickpeas, eggs, coconut oil, honey, cocoa powder, espresso powder (if using), baking powder, and baking soda. Blend or process until smooth. Transfer to the prepared pan and stir in the chocolate chips by hand. 4. Set the pan in the air fryer basket and bake for 20 minutes, or until a toothpick inserted into the center comes out clean. 5. Let cool in the pan on a wire rack for 30 minutes before cutting into squares. 6. Serve immediately.

Cream-Filled Sponge Cakes

Prep time: 10 minutes | Cook time: 10 minutes | Makes 4 cakes

Coconut, or avocado oil, for spraying

1 tube croissant dough

4 cream-filled sponge cake fingers

1 tablespoon icing sugar

1. Line the air fryer basket with baking paper, and spray lightly with oil. 2. Unroll the dough into a single flat layer and cut it into 4 equal pieces. 3. Place 1 sponge cake in the center of each piece of dough. Wrap the dough around the cake, pinching the ends to seal. 4. Place the wrapped cakes in the prepared basket, and spray lightly with oil. 5. Bake at 90ºC for 5 minutes, flip, spray with oil, and cook for another 5 minutes, or until golden brown. 6. Dust with the icing sugar and serve.

Gingerbread

Prep time: 5 minutes | Cook time: 20 minutes | Makes 1 loaf

Cooking spray

125 g plain flour

2 tablespoons granulated sugar

¾ teaspoon ground ginger

¼ teaspoon cinnamon

1 teaspoon baking powder

½ teaspoon baking soda

⅛ teaspoon salt

1 egg

70 g treacle

120 ml buttermilk

2 tablespoons coconut, or avocado oil

1 teaspoon pure vanilla extract

1. Preheat the air fryer to 165ºC. 2. Spray a baking dish lightly with cooking spray. 3. In a medium bowl, mix together all the dry ingredients. 4. In a separate bowl, beat the egg. Add treacle, buttermilk, oil, and vanilla and stir until well mixed. 5. Pour liquid mixture into dry ingredients and stir until well blended. 6. Pour batter into baking dish and bake for 20 minutes, or until toothpick inserted in center of loaf comes out clean.

Breaded Bananas with Chocolate Topping

Prep time: 10 minutes | Cook time: 10 minutes | Serves 6

40 g cornflour	3 bananas, halved crosswise
25 g plain breadcrumbs	Cooking spray
1 large egg, beaten	Chocolate sauce, for serving

1. Preheat the air fryer to 175°C. 2. Place the cornflour, breadcrumbs, and egg in three separate bowls. 3. Roll the bananas in the cornstarch, then in the beaten egg, and finally in the breadcrumbs to coat well. 4. Spritz the air fryer basket with the cooking spray. 5. Arrange the banana halves in the basket and mist them with the cooking spray. Air fry for 5 minutes. Flip the bananas and continue to air fry for another 2 minutes. 6. Remove the bananas from the basket to a serving plate. Serve with the chocolate sauce drizzled over the top.

Chocolate Bread Pudding

Prep time: 10 minutes | Cook time: 10 to 12 minutes | Serves 4

Nonstick, flour-infused baking spray	2 tablespoons cocoa powder
1 egg	3 tablespoons light brown sugar
1 egg yolk	3 tablespoons peanut butter
175 ml chocolate milk	1 teaspoon vanilla extract
	5 slices firm white bread, cubed

1. Spray a 6-by-2-inch round baking pan with the baking spray. Set aside. 2. In a medium bowl, whisk the egg, egg yolk, chocolate milk, cocoa powder, brown sugar, peanut butter, and vanilla until thoroughly combined. Stir in the bread cubes and let soak for 10 minutes. Spoon this mixture into the prepared pan. 3. Insert the crisper plate into the basket and the basket into the unit. Preheat the unit to 165°C. 4. cook the pudding for about 10 minutes and then check if done. It is done when it is firm to the touch. If not, resume cooking. 5. When the cooking is complete, let the pudding cool for 5 minutes. Serve warm.

Chocolate Chip Pecan Biscotti

Prep time: 15 minutes | Cook time: 20 to 22 minutes | Serves 10

135 g finely ground blanched almond flour	1 large egg, beaten
¾ teaspoon baking powder	1 teaspoon pure vanilla extract
½ teaspoon xanthan gum	50 g chopped pecans
¼ teaspoon sea salt	40 g organic chocolate chips,
3 tablespoons unsalted butter, at room temperature	Melted organic chocolate chips and chopped pecans, for topping (optional)
35 g powdered sweetener	

1. In a large bowl, combine the almond flour, baking powder, xanthan gum, and salt. 2. Line a cake pan that fits inside your air fryer with baking paper. 3. In the bowl of a stand mixer, beat together the butter and powdered sweetener. Add the beaten egg and vanilla and beat for about 3 minutes. 4. Add the almond flour mixture to the butter and egg mixture; beat until just combined. 5. Stir in the pecans and chocolate chips. 6. Transfer the dough to the prepared pan and press it into the bottom. 7. Set the air fryer to 165°C and bake for 12 minutes. Remove from the air fryer and let cool for 15 minutes. Using a sharp knife, cut the cookie into thin strips, then return the strips to the cake pan with the bottom sides facing up. 8. Set the air fryer to 150°C. Bake for 8 to 10 minutes. 9. Remove from the air fryer and let cool completely on a wire rack. If desired, dip one side of each biscotti piece into melted chocolate chips, and top with chopped pecans.

Cinnamon and Pecan Pie

Prep time: 10 minutes | Cook time: 25 minutes | Serves 4

1 pack shortcrust pastry	⅛ teaspoon nutmeg
½ teaspoons cinnamon	3 tablespoons melted butter,
¾ teaspoon vanilla extract	divided
2 eggs	2 tablespoons sugar
175 ml maple syrup	65 g chopped pecans

1. Preheat the air fryer to 190°C. 2. In a small bowl, coat the pecans in 1 tablespoon of melted butter. 3. Transfer the pecans to the air fryer and air fry for about 10 minutes. 4. Put the pie dough in a greased pie pan, trim off the excess and add the pecans on top. 5. In a bowl, mix the rest of the ingredients. Pour this over the pecans. 6. Put the pan in the air fryer and bake for 25 minutes. 7. Serve immediately.

Baked Peaches with Yogurt and Blueberries

Prep time: 10 minutes | Cook time: 7 to 11 minutes | Serves 6

3 peaches, peeled, halved, and pitted	285 g plain Greek yogurt
2 tablespoons packed brown sugar	¼ teaspoon ground cinnamon
	1 teaspoon pure vanilla extract
	190 g fresh blueberries

1. Preheat the air fryer to 190°C. 2. Arrange the peaches in the air fryer basket, cut side up. Top with a generous sprinkle of brown sugar. 3. Bake in the preheated air fryer for 7 to 11 minutes, or until the peaches are lightly browned and caramelized. 4. Meanwhile, whisk together the yogurt, cinnamon, and vanilla in a small bowl until smooth. 5. Remove the peaches from the basket to a plate. Serve topped with the yogurt mixture and fresh blueberries.

Indian Toast and Milk

Prep time: 10 minutes | Cook time: 20 minutes | Serves 4

305 g sweetened, condensed milk

240 ml evaporated milk

240 ml single cream

1 teaspoon ground cardamom, plus additional for garnish

1 pinch saffron threads

4 slices white bread

2 to 3 tablespoons ghee or butter, softened

2 tablespoons crushed pistachios, for garnish (optional)

1. In a baking pan, combine the condensed milk, evaporated milk, half-and-half, cardamom, and saffron. Stir until well combined. 2. Place the pan in the air fryer basket. Set the air fryer to 175ºC for 15 minutes, stirring halfway through the cooking time. Remove the sweetened milk from the air fryer and set aside. 3. Cut each slice of bread into two triangles. Brush each side with ghee. Place the bread in the air fryer basket. Keeping the air fryer on 175ºC cook for 5 minutes or until golden brown and toasty. 4. Remove the bread from the air fryer. Arrange two triangles in each of four wide, shallow bowls. Pour the hot milk mixture on top of the bread and let soak for 30 minutes. 5. Garnish with pistachios if using, and sprinkle with additional cardamom.

Air Fryer Apple Fritters

Prep time: 30 minutes | Cook time: 7 to 8 minutes | Serves 6

1 chopped, peeled Granny Smith apple

115 g granulated sugar

1 teaspoon ground cinnamon

120 g plain flour

1 teaspoon baking powder

1 teaspoon salt

2 tablespoons milk

2 tablespoons butter, melted

1 large egg, beaten

Cooking spray

25 g icing sugar (optional)

1. Mix together the apple, granulated sugar, and cinnamon in a small bowl. Allow to sit for 30 minutes. 2. Combine the flour, baking powder, and salt in a medium bowl. Add the milk, butter, and egg and stir to incorporate. 3. Pour the apple mixture into the bowl of flour mixture and stir with a spatula until a dough forms. 4. Make the fritters: On a clean work surface, divide the dough into 12 equal portions and shape into 1-inch balls. Flatten them into patties with your hands. 5. Preheat the air fryer to 175ºC. Line the air fryer basket with baking paper and spray it with cooking spray. 6. Transfer the apple fritters onto the baking paper, evenly spaced but not too close together. Spray the fritters with cooking spray. 7. Bake for 7 to 8 minutes until lightly browned. Flip the fritters halfway through the cooking time. 8. Remove from the basket to a plate and serve with the confectioners' sugar sprinkled on top, if desired.

Protein Powder Doughnut Holes

Prep time: 25 minutes | Cook time: 6 minutes | Makes 12 holes

50 g blanched finely ground almond flour

60 g low-carb vanilla protein powder

100 g granulated sweetener

½ teaspoon baking powder

1 large egg

5 tablespoons unsalted butter, melted

½ teaspoon vanilla extract

1. Mix all ingredients in a large bowl. Place into the freezer for 20 minutes. 2. Wet your hands with water and roll the dough into twelve balls. 3. Cut a piece of baking paper to fit your air fryer basket. Working in batches as necessary, place doughnut holes into the air fryer basket on top of baking paper. 4. Adjust the temperature to 190ºC and air fry for 6 minutes. 5. Flip doughnut holes halfway through the cooking time. 6. Let cool completely before serving.

Blackberry Cobbler

Prep time: 15 minutes | Cook time: 25 to 30 minutes | Serves 6

330 g fresh or frozen blackberries

350 g granulated sugar, divided into 200 g and 150 g

1 teaspoon vanilla extract

8 tablespoons butter, melted

125 g self-raising flour

1 to 2 tablespoons oil

1. In a medium bowl, stir together the blackberries, 200 g of sugar, and vanilla. 2. In another medium bowl, stir together the melted butter, remaining 150 g of sugar, and flour until a dough forms. 3. Spritz a baking pan with oil. Add the blackberry mixture. Crumble the flour mixture over the fruit. Cover the pan with aluminum foil. 4. Preheat the air fryer to 175ºC. 5. Place the covered pan in the air fryer basket. Cook for 20 to 25 minutes until the filling is thickened. 6. Uncover the pan and cook for 5 minutes more, depending on how juicy and browned you like your cobbler. Let sit for 5 minutes before serving.

Coconut Muffins

Prep time: 5 minutes | Cook time: 25 minutes | Serves 5

55 g coconut flour

2 tablespoons cocoa powder

3 tablespoons granulated sweetener

1 teaspoon baking powder

2 tablespoons coconut oil

2 eggs, beaten

50 g desiccated coconut

1. In the mixing bowl, mix all ingredients. 2. Then pour the mixture into the molds of the muffin and transfer in the air fryer basket. 3. Cook the muffins at 175ºC for 25 minutes.

Fried Cheesecake Bites

Prep time: 30 minutes | Cook time: 2 minutes | Makes 16 bites

225 g cream cheese, softened

50 g powdered sweetener, plus 2 tablespoons, divided

4 tablespoons heavy cream,

divided

½ teaspoon vanilla extract

50 g almond flour

1. In a stand mixer fitted with a paddle attachment, beat the cream cheese, 50 g of the sweetener, 2 tablespoons of the heavy cream, and the vanilla until smooth. Using a small ice-cream scoop, divide the mixture into 16 balls and arrange them on a rimmed baking sheet lined with baking paper. Freeze for 45 minutes until firm. 2. Line the air fryer basket with baking paper and preheat the air fryer to 175ºC. 3. In a small shallow bowl, combine the almond flour with the remaining 2 tablespoons of sweetener. 4. In another small shallow bowl, place the remaining 2 tablespoons cream. 5. One at a time, dip the frozen cheesecake balls into the cream and then roll in the almond flour mixture, pressing lightly to form an even coating. Arrange the balls in a single layer in the air fryer basket, leaving room between them. Air fry for 2 minutes until the coating is lightly browned.

Pumpkin-Spice Bread Pudding

Prep time: 15 minutes | Cook time: 35 minutes | Serves 6

Bread Pudding:

175 ml heavy whipping cream

120 g canned pumpkin

80 ml whole milk

65 g granulated sugar

1 large egg plus 1 yolk

½ teaspoon pumpkin pie spice

⅛ teaspoon kosher, or coarse sea salt

1/3 loaf of day-old baguette or crusty country bread, cubed

4 tablespoons unsalted butter, melted

Sauce:

80 ml pure maple syrup

1 tablespoon unsalted butter

120 ml heavy whipping cream

½ teaspoon pure vanilla extract

1. For the bread pudding: In a medium bowl, combine the cream, pumpkin, milk, sugar, egg and yolk, pumpkin pie spice, and salt. Whisk until well combined. 2. In a large bowl, toss the bread cubes with the melted butter. Add the pumpkin mixture and gently toss until the ingredients are well combined. 3. Transfer the mixture to a baking pan. Place the pan in the air fryer basket. Set the fryer to 175ºC cooking for 35 minutes, or until custard is set in the middle. 4. Meanwhile, for the sauce: In a small saucepan, combine the syrup and butter. Heat over medium heat, stirring, until the butter melts. Stir in the cream and simmer, stirring often, until the sauce has thickened, about 15 minutes. Stir in the vanilla. Remove the pudding from the air fryer. 5. Let the pudding stand for 10 minutes before serving with the warm sauce.

Rhubarb and Strawberry Crumble

Prep time: 10 minutes | Cook time: 12 to 17 minutes | Serves 6

250 g sliced fresh strawberries

95 g sliced rhubarb

75 g granulated sugar

60 g quick-cooking oatmeal

50 g whole-wheat pastry flour,

or plain flour

50 g packed light brown sugar

½ teaspoon ground cinnamon

3 tablespoons unsalted butter, melted

1. Insert the crisper plate into the basket and the basket into the unit. Preheat the unit to 190ºC. 2. In a 6-by-2-inch round metal baking pan, combine the strawberries, rhubarb, and granulated sugar. 3. In a medium bowl, stir together the oatmeal, flour, brown sugar, and cinnamon. Stir the melted butter into this mixture until crumbly. Sprinkle the crumble mixture over the fruit. 4. Once the unit is preheated, place the pan into the basket. 5. Bake for 12 minutes then check the crumble. If the fruit is bubbling and the topping is golden brown, it is done. If not, resume cooking. 6. When the cooking is complete, serve warm.

Pineapple Galette

Prep time: 15 minutes | Cook time: 40 minutes | Serves 2

¼ medium-size pineapple, peeled, cored, and cut crosswise into ¼-inch-thick slices

2 tablespoons dark rum, or apple juice

1 teaspoon vanilla extract

½ teaspoon kosher, or coarse sea salt

Finely grated zest of ½ lime

1 store-bought sheet puff pastry, cut into an 8-inch round

3 tablespoons granulated sugar

2 tablespoons unsalted butter, cubed and chilled

Coconut ice cream, for serving

1. In a small bowl, combine the pineapple slices, rum, vanilla, salt, and lime zest and let stand for at least 10 minutes to allow the pineapple to soak in the rum. 2. Meanwhile, press the puff pastry round into the bottom and up the sides of a cake pan and use the tines of a fork to dock the bottom and sides. 3. Arrange the pineapple slices on the bottom of the pastry in a more or less single layer, then sprinkle with the sugar and dot with the butter. Drizzle with the leftover juices from the bowl. Place the pan in the air fryer and bake at 155ºC until the pastry is puffed and golden brown and the pineapple is lightly caramelized on top, about 40 minutes. 4. Transfer the pan to a wire rack to cool for 15 minutes. Unmold the galette from the pan and serve warm with coconut ice cream.

Vanilla Cookies with Hazelnuts

Prep time: 20 minutes | Cook time: 10 minutes | Serves 6

110 g almond flour

55 g coconut flour

1 teaspoon baking soda

1 teaspoon fine sea salt

110 g unsalted butter

120 g powdered sweetener

2 teaspoons vanilla

2 eggs, at room temperature

130 g hazelnuts, coarsely chopped

1. Preheat the air fryer to 175°C. 2. Mix the flour with the baking soda, and sea salt. 3. In the bowl of an electric mixer, beat the butter, sweetener, and vanilla until creamy. Fold in the eggs, one at a time, and mix until well combined. 4. Slowly and gradually, stir in the flour mixture. Finally, fold in the coarsely chopped hazelnuts. 5. Divide the dough into small balls using a large cookie scoop; drop onto the prepared cookie sheets. Bake for 10 minutes or until golden brown, rotating the pan once or twice through the cooking time. 6. Work in batches and cool for a couple of minutes before removing to wire racks. Enjoy!

Printed in Great Britain
by Amazon

17470101R00038